AF411813

KEVIN BEASLEY

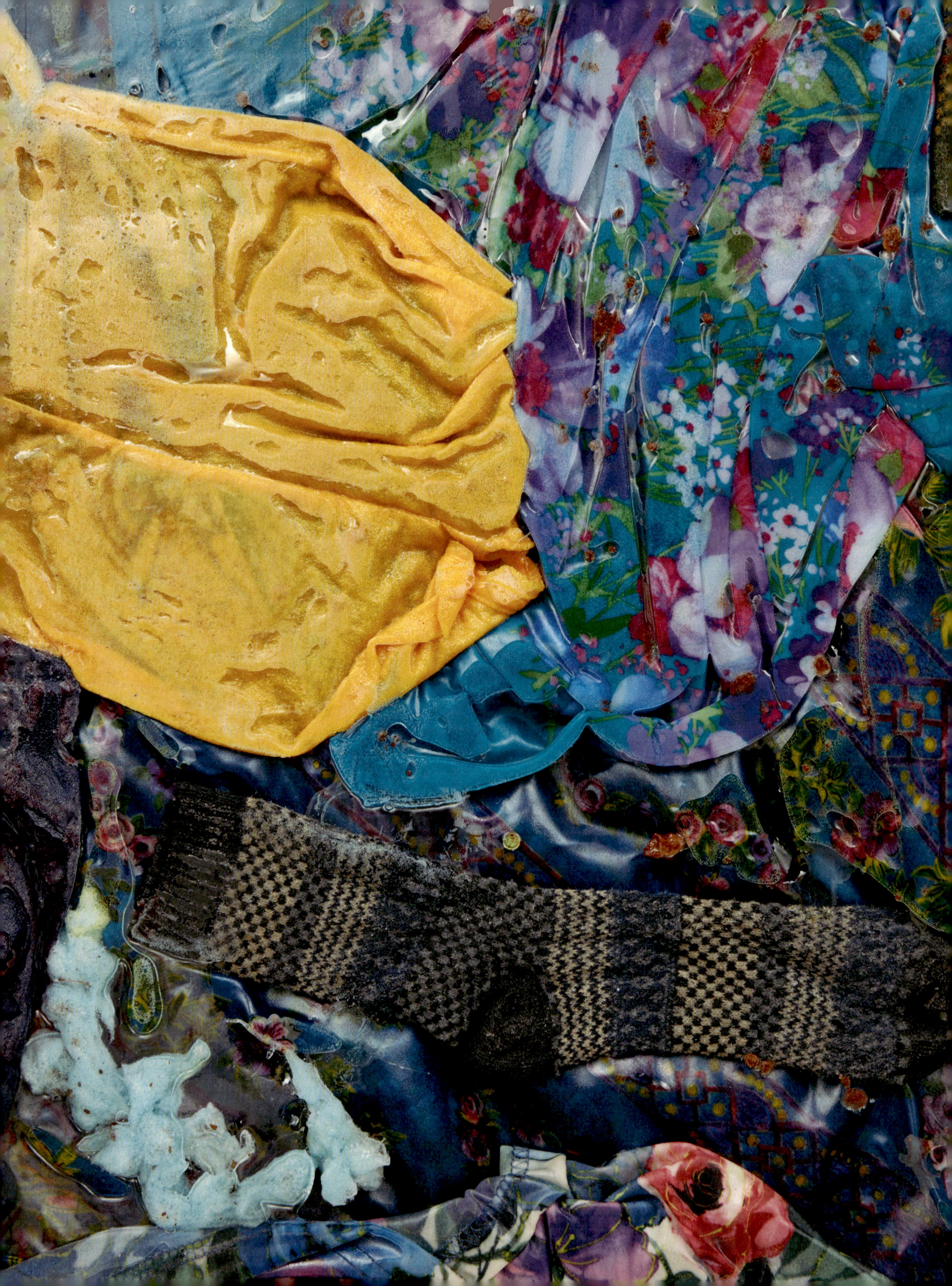

KEVIN BEASLEY

Ruth Erickson

The Institute of Contemporary Art/Boston

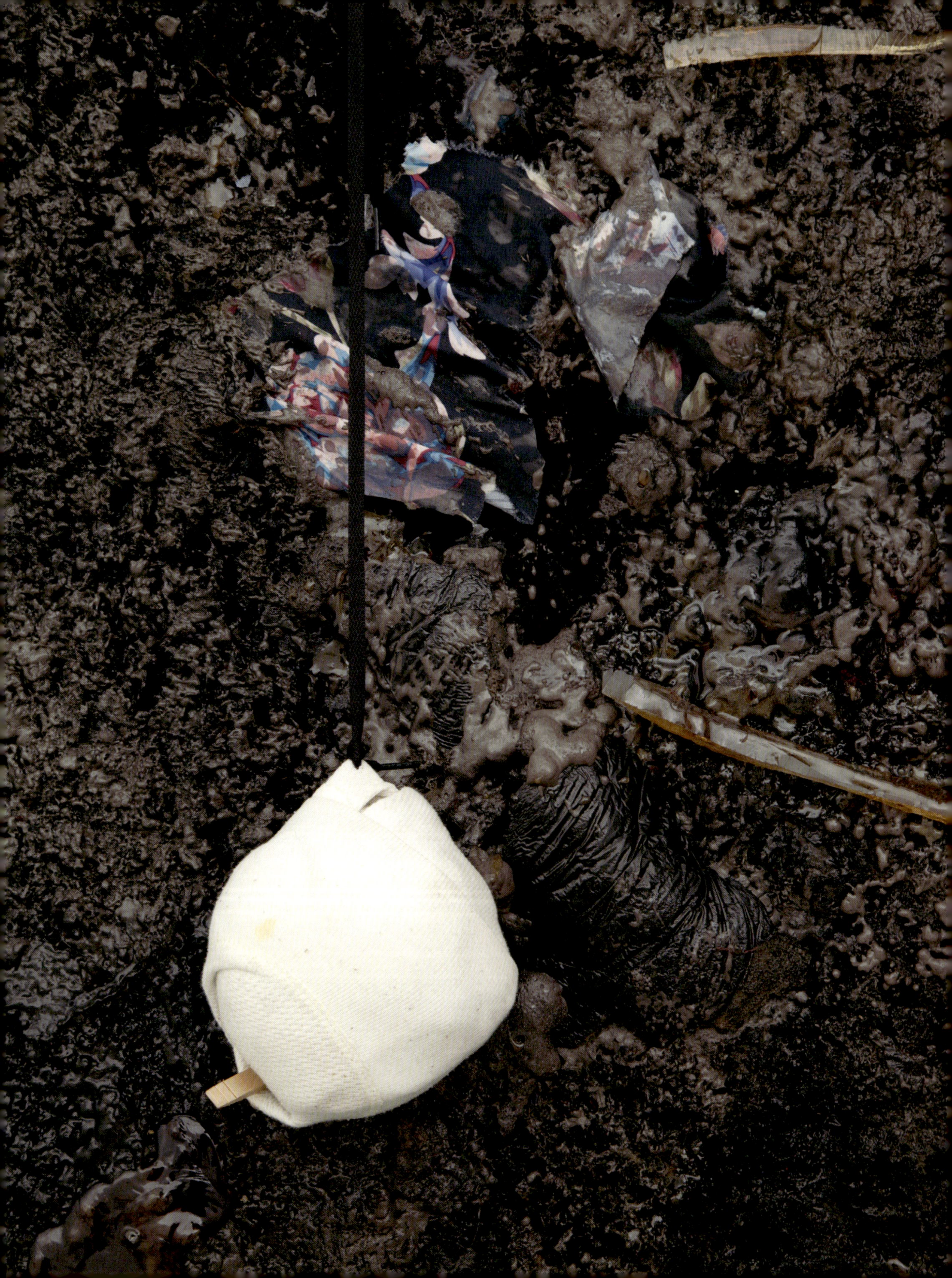

Contents

Director's Foreword

Sights and sounds are the stuff of dreams and memories—the lived experiences that materialize as fragmented images and reverberations in our personal and collective histories. Kevin Beasley takes his inspiration from the visual and aural landscapes of his childhood in the American South; the cars, design, and history of Detroit; and the artistic exposure and influences of Los Angeles and New York, and transforms them into the disembodied and provocative sculptures and soundtracks that characterize his art.

Visually, Beasley's is an art of timeworn clothing and artifacts immortalized by resin, sometimes on canvas, sometimes freestanding: housedresses and kaftans, socks and sneakers, bandanas and hats, molded, folded, shaped, and fixed into works of art. Via satellite dishes, microphones, speakers, cables, and television mounts, Beasley uses the language of music and spoken word to excavate and amplify his landscape through sound.

The ICA is very proud to present Kevin Beasley's first major solo museum exhibition. Situated in a tradition of contemporary art that elevates found objects, household remnants, and vernacular materials, Beasley references, in particular, artists David Hammons, Noah Purifoy, Senga Nengudi, and Melvin Edwards—black artists, long marginalized in contemporary art history, who chart distinct African American histories and economies, and whose utilization of assemblage and mixed media speaks loudly of ruin, rebellion, reclamation, and race. Beasely's practice continues in this tradition in his unique voice, connecting home and street, private and public, and visual and performance idioms and identities.

We are grateful to Ruth Erickson, Mannion Family Curator, for bringing this idea, exhibition, and book forward, and for her unwavering commitment to art and justice. Ruth was ably assisted by Jeffrey De Blois, Assistant Curator, and the ICA staff.

For their generosity in helping realize this exhibition, we greatly appreciate Fotene Demoulas and Tom Coté, The Coby Foundation, Ltd., Bernard Lumpkin and Carmine Boccuzzi, Casey Kaplan gallery, the lenders to the exhibition, and the ICA board and staff.

Finally, for the opportunity to support and share his work with our audiences, we thank Kevin Beasley for partnering with us on this exhibition and publication, and for the opportunity to share his vision and his work with our public.

Jill Medvedow
Ellen Matilda Poss Director

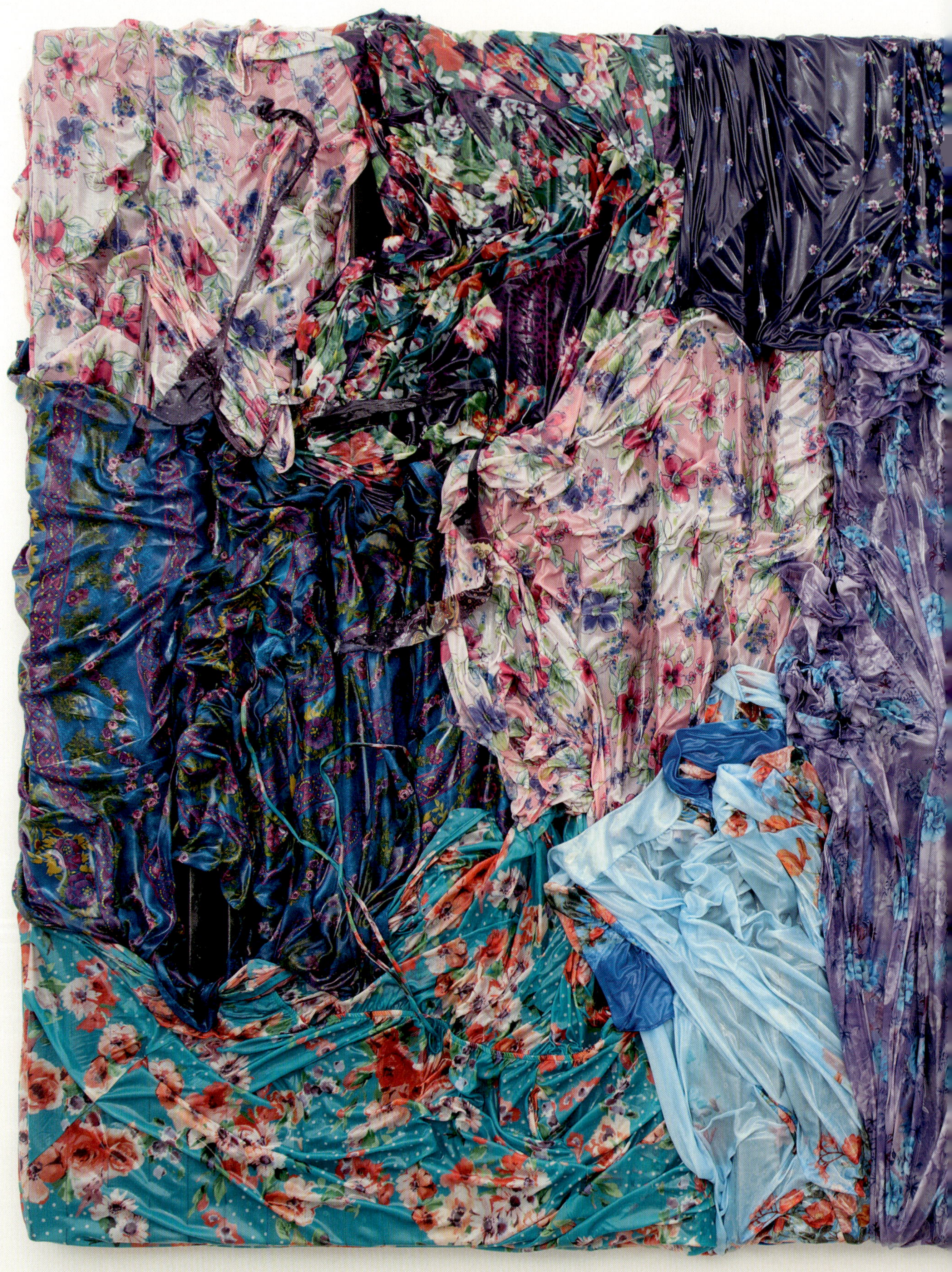

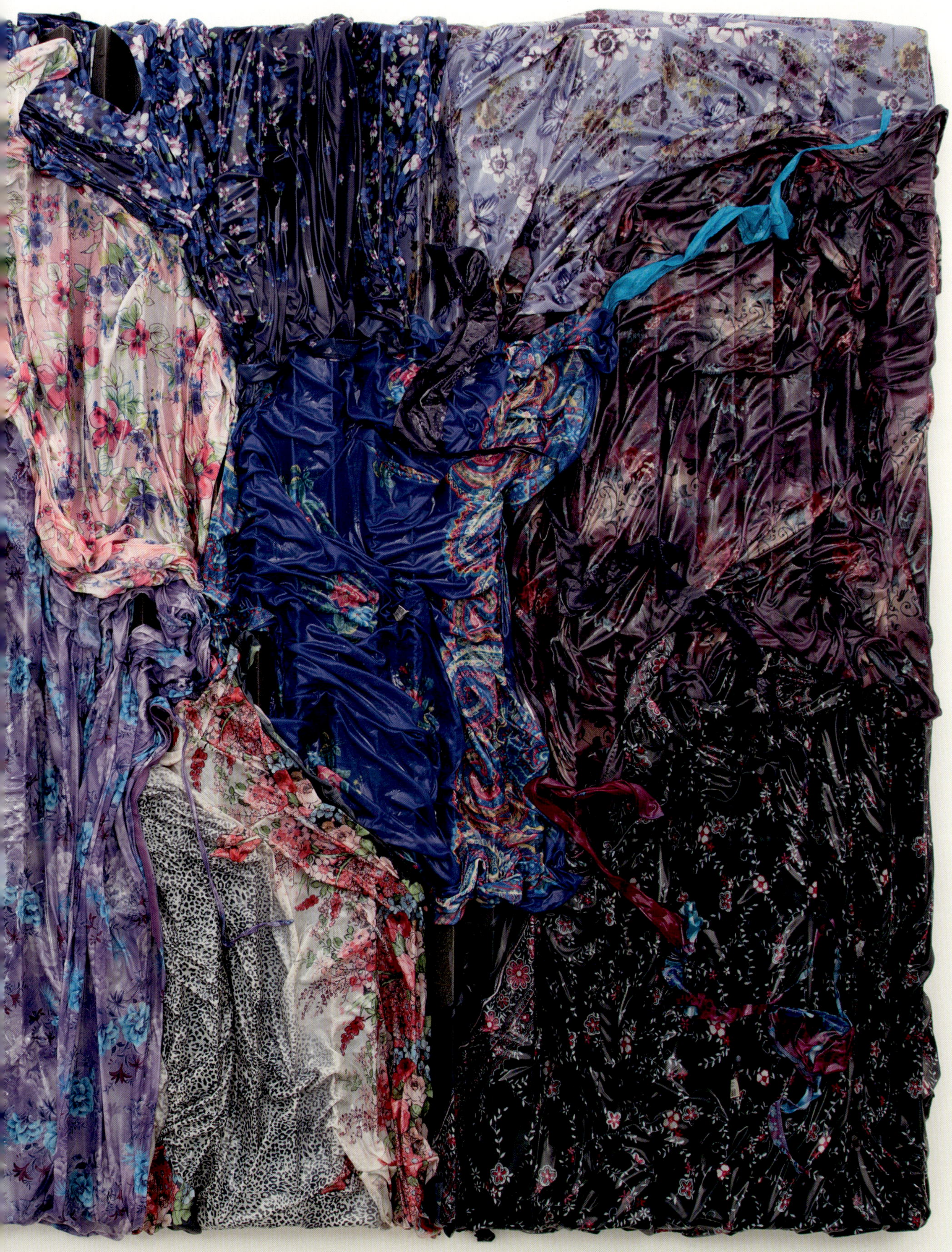

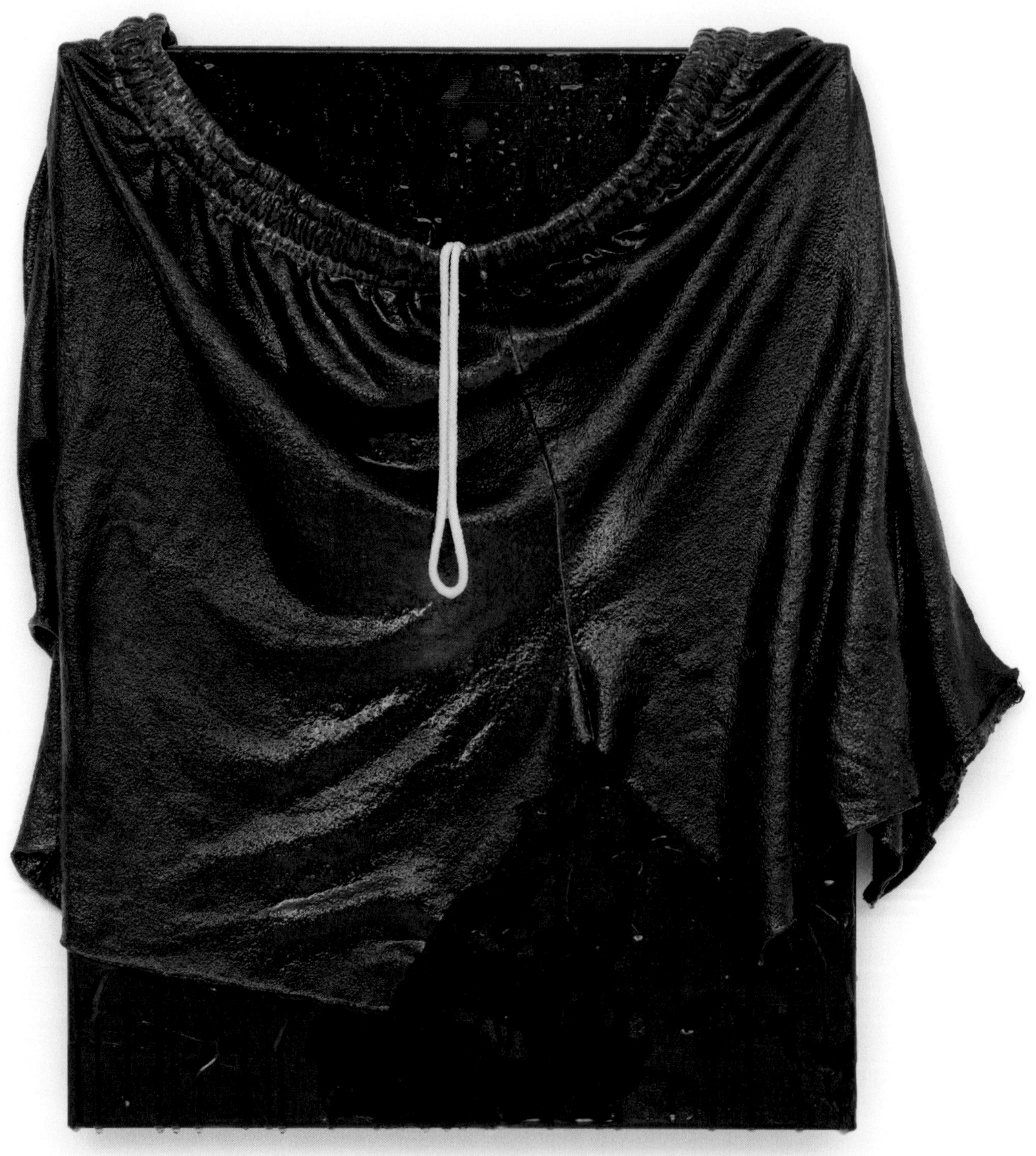

Objects of Consequence

Ruth Erickson

In America, it is traditional to destroy the black body—
it is heritage. Enslavement was not merely the antiseptic
borrowing of labor—it is not so easy to get a human being
to commit their body against its own elemental interest.
And so enslavement must be casual wrath and random
manglings, the gashing of heads and brains blown out over
the river as the body seeks to escape. It must be rape so
regular as to be industrial. There is no uplifting way to say
this. I have no praise anthems, nor old Negro spirituals.
The spirit and soul are the body and brain, which are
destructible—that is precisely why they are so precious.
　　　　　　　　 –Ta-Nehisi Coates, *Between the World and Me*

There's a process by which bodies blend in, or don't, or
die, or roll on past the siren's glow so as not to subpoena
the grave.

　　　　　　　　　 –Joshua Bennett, *The Sobbing School*

American history is a history of traumatic and blatant erasures of black
subjects through perniciously visible, durable, and interconnected
systems, including the transatlantic slave trade, centuries of enslavement, lynching and public murders, the industrial prison system, and

Previous: *Untitled (Monday)*,
2016. Housedresses, kaftans,
altered bandanas, du-rags,
altered kente fabric, resin, wood,
and acoustic foam. 78 x 126 x
7 inches (198.1 x 320 x 17.8 cm).
San Francisco Museum
of Modern Art, Accessions
Committee Fund purchase.

Untitled, 2016. Resin and
altered sweatpants on canvas.
24¾ x 23¾ x 3½ inches
(62.9 x 60.3 x 8.9 cm). Private
collection, Boston.

institutional racism. While ranging widely in form and structure, the bodies alluded to in Kevin Beasley's recent artistic production have been anchored in his exploration of black experiences. His practice has emerged during a period of heightened awareness among whites, myself included, of the destruction of black bodies in America, as so powerfully articulated by the contemporary writers Ta-Nehisi Coates, Saidiya Hartman, and Christina Sharpe, among many others, and by the Black Lives Matter movement.

In Beasley's work, bodies are rarely whole or complete, but rather are envisaged in indeterminate and interconnected states. Sometimes the bodies are "spectral" ones, those of deceased rappers or murdered teens; absences are metaphorically presented in the form of a dented surface or the image of a field in the South at sunset. At other times, the bodies are very particular, and even enumerated as personal objects that figure in his artworks: "That is my thermal shirt . . . my underwear . . . my old sneakers . . . my brother's wisdom teeth." And then there are the listeners and viewers who share space with Beasley's performances, sculptures, and installations, and who are always present in the conception of his work. Beasley conjures these bodies and their states of being through various strategies, from selecting objects and manipulating materials to activating space through sound and installation. Each gesture underscores the ethics of his artistic practice—his respect for the power and responsibility of bringing an artwork into the world that requires space, resources, and care.

The material core of Beasley's sculptures and installations is formed by a broad range of objects: baseball caps, du-rags, jackets, dresses, shoes, rugs, chairs, sports equipment, and gas masks, among many other things, recur in his work. The artist carefully selects and repurposes common and familiar items—some of which are store-bought and new, others are used or the artist's own belongings. He uses them as raw materials, drawing on their symbolism as he transforms them into artworks and, in the process, imbues them with new meanings. As such, the existence of these objects in physical space contains deeper meaning in social, political, and psychic space. Meanings then become highly dynamic, evolving over time, from the moment of an object's initial commercial production to Beasley's performative moments of use and reuse, to the reproduction and recirculation of meaning within artworks.

Beasley has a keen sense for how objects engender meaning, and for the possibilities found through relationships and juxtapositions

Billy's Clubs, 2017. Resin, polyurethane foam, seashells, golf clubs, golf bag, and billy club. 67 x 28 x 10 inches (170.2 x 71.1 x 25.4 cm). Private collection, London. Photo by Jason Wyche.

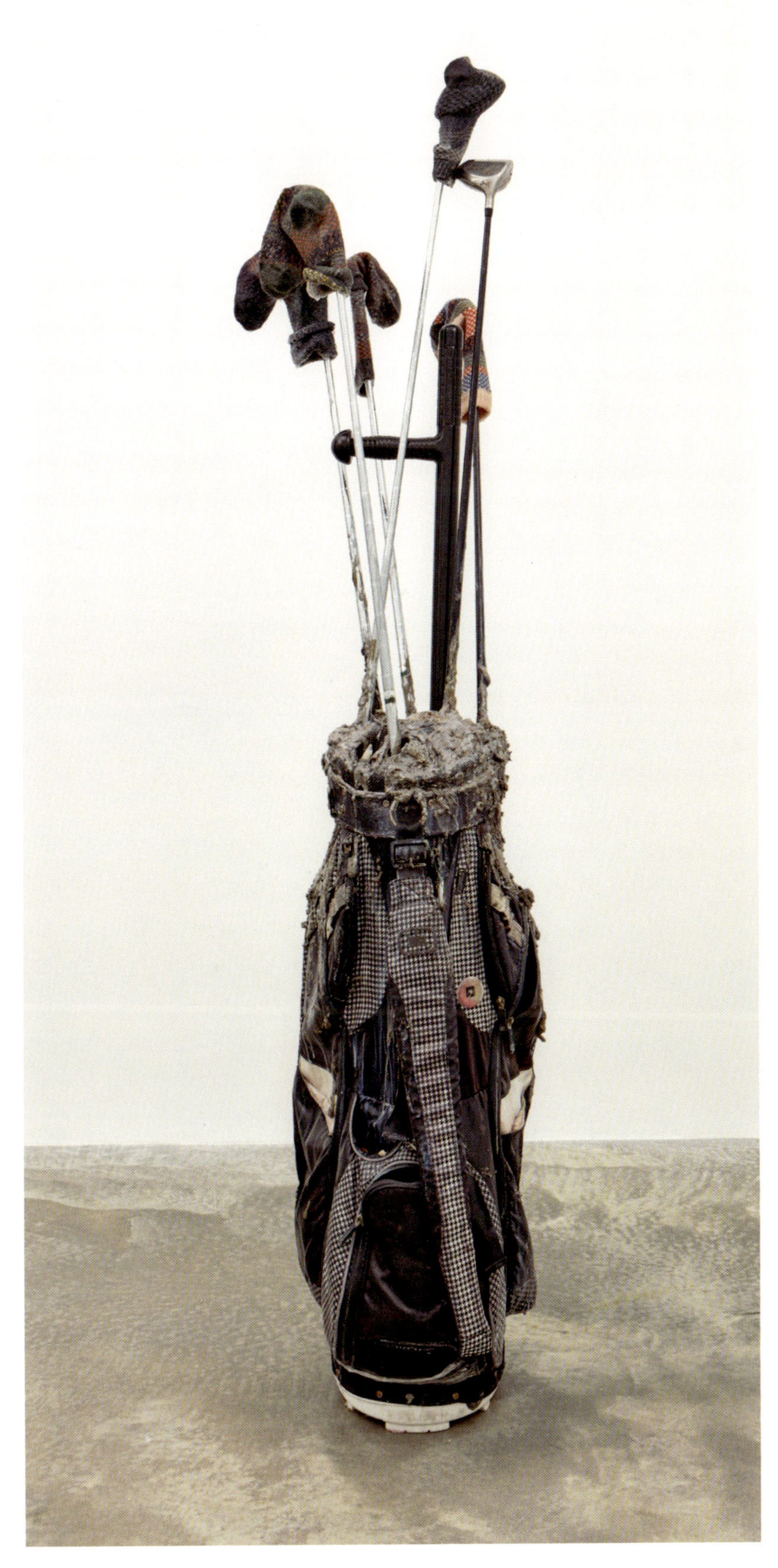

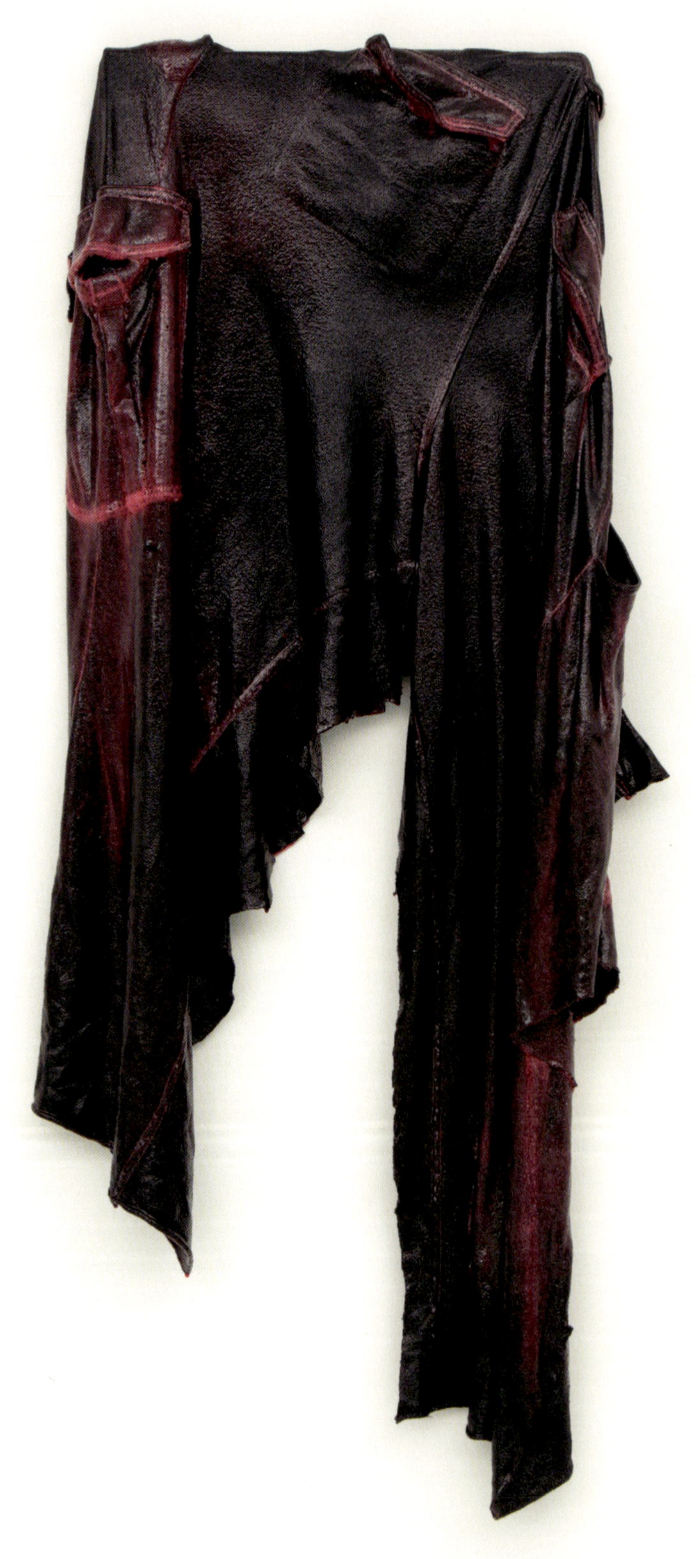

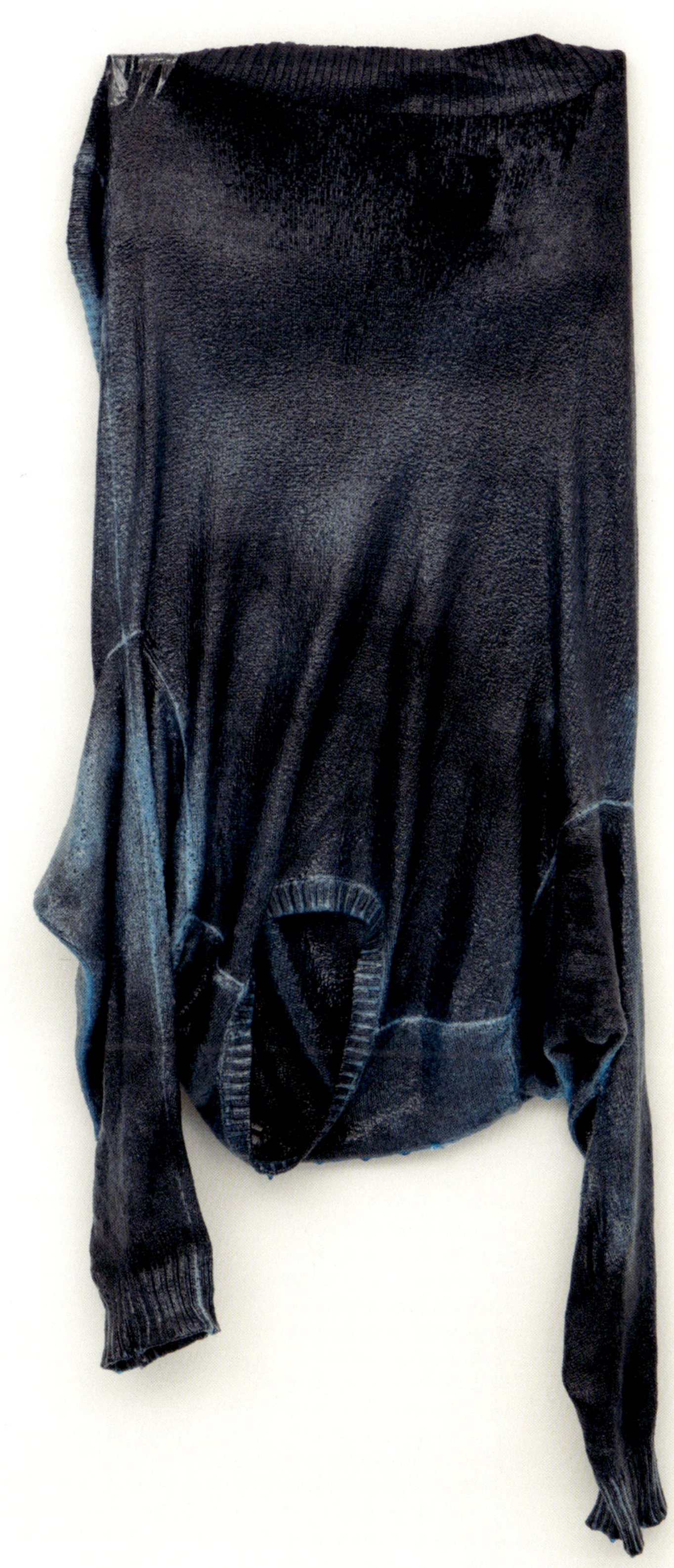

within specific communities or cultures—as in theorist Stuart Hall's formulation,[1] the linked operations of "encoding" and "decoding." Take, for example, the material most closely associated with the artist's recent output: colorful polyester housedresses. As Beasley tells the story, it was during the summer before his residency at the Studio Museum in Harlem (2013–14) that he visited a dress shop on 116th Street in New York City.[2] He remembered going to this very same shop with his grandmother and aunt to buy dresses on his childhood visits to New York City from Virginia. The shop, which used to stand across from where his mother's family lived, has been in operation since 1952, with the same family selling the same quality dresses at affordable prices.

The store's owner, Fred Abi-Hassoun, son of the founding couple, Elias and Olga, has said that his retail shop also functions as a community space, holding together the threads of the neighborhood and serving people who live there in a rapidly gentrifying and always changing landscape.[3] On Fridays and Saturdays, women pour into the store to buy brightly colored, loose-fitting dresses in polyester and cotton

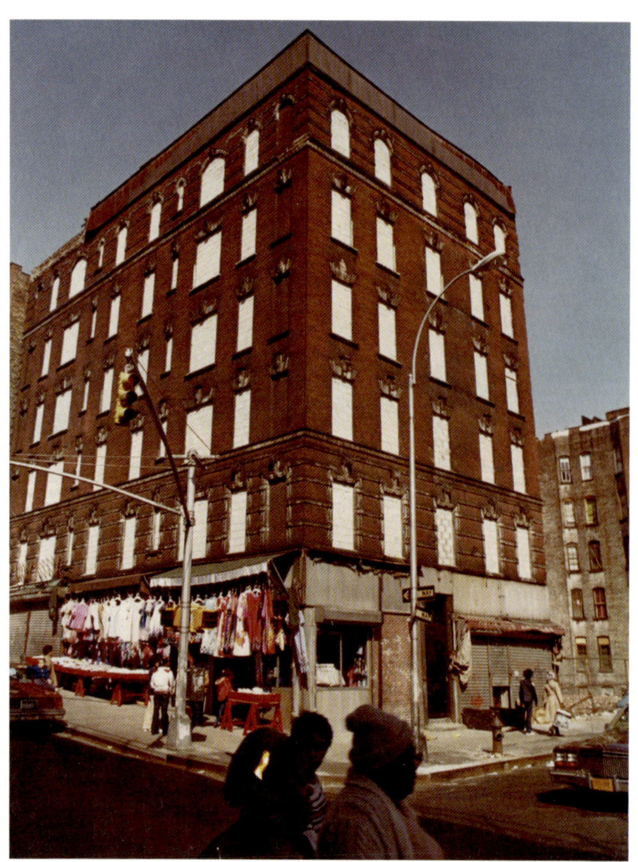

Dress shop on 116th Street in Harlem, c. 1980. Photo courtesy the archives of George and Fred Abi-Hassoun.

Opposite: *Untitled (Look)* (rear view), 2015. Housedresses and resin. 38 x 28 x 10 inches (96.5 x 71.1 x 25.4 cm). Collection of Jennifer and David Stockman, New York.

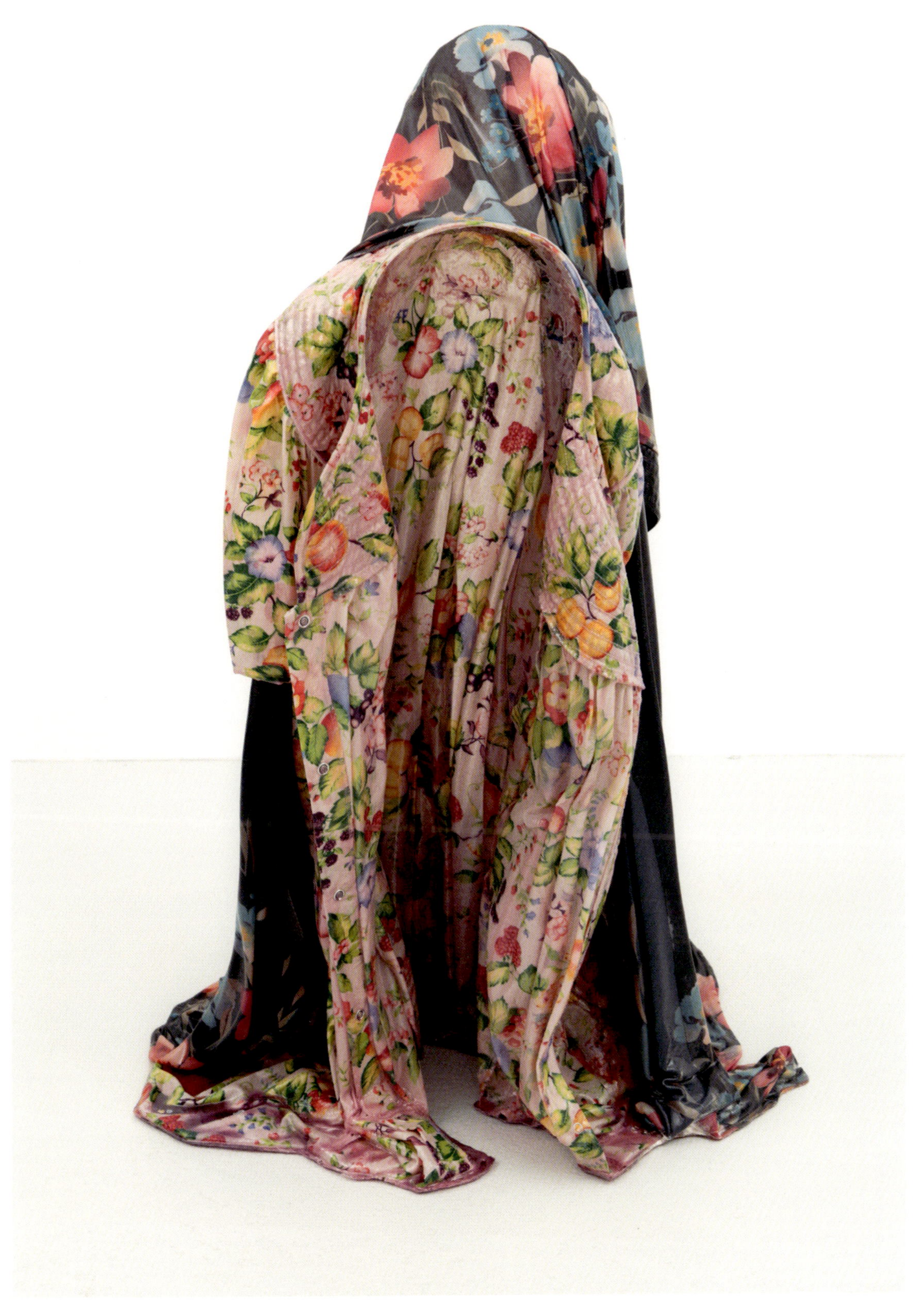

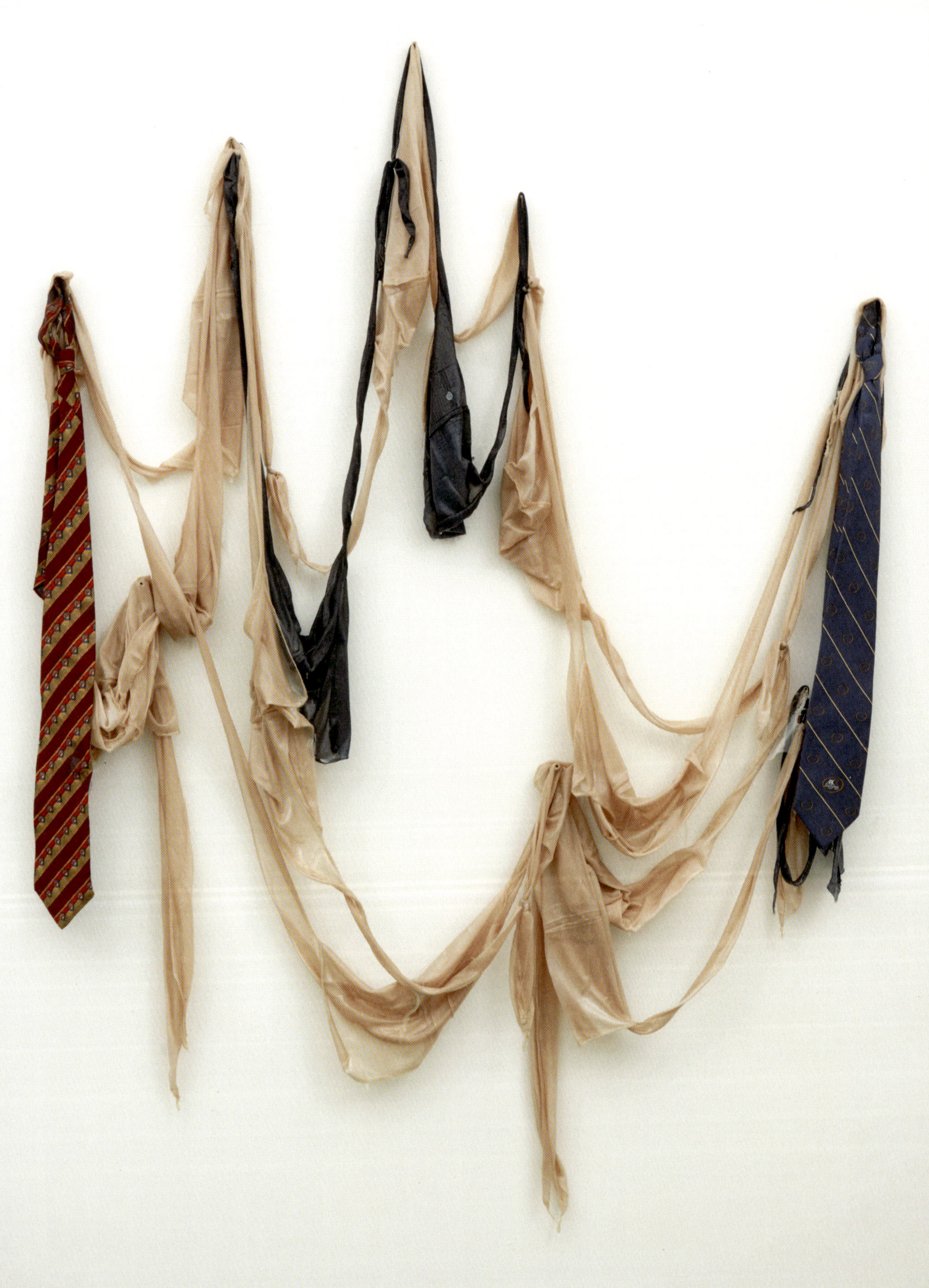

for roughly twelve dollars each. As such, the store has a warm and very human atmosphere, and the fact that it is still thriving suggests a bygone era of New York, when lower- and middle-income working people could see the city as a place of possibility. Beasley started buying dresses from this shop in 2013 because the shop and the dresses have a connection to his family history and to his first encounters with New York (which, since 2012, has been his home). The store's owner describes Beasley as "a very good friend," and the artist regularly returns to the shop to fill the metal racks in his studio with Abi-Hassoun's colorfully patterned dresses, which he will make into sculptures that now figure in some of the country's most prominent museum collections. In choosing to work with the polyester housedresses, Beasley joins the strong matriarchs in his young life—his memories of them and of New York City, the housing development where they lived, and the store that supplied these women with affordable clothes—with his labor and effort as an artist, working to make sculptures that matter and that are worth preserving. This circuit functions like a kind of fortress against the relentless social, economic, and physical attacks on civility, respectability, community, and care. Abi-Hassoun characterized Beasley's artworks as "giving voice to a way of life."[4]

Air Jordan and Nike sneakers, du-rags, and hoodies also frequently appear in Beasley's sculptures, items that possess immediate and layered connections to American black culture. Take, for example, the pair of NIke Air Jordans in *Untitled (Jumped Man)* (2014). Coveted by youth, these sneakers are cited in rap lyrics such as "I stay sportin' played Jordan's before Jordan / Verses tight, hooks harder than Ken Norton" by Jay-Z,[5] and the shoes have been at times known to incite schoolyard and neighborhood brawls. The title of the sculpture is a play on words, combining a reference to the sneaker's iconic "Jumpman" logo with the violent experience of getting jumped or robbed. Beasley has attached purplish-gray industrial foam to the white, black, and purple sneakers; the bulbous forms appear like chunks of rock, or tumors. The foam has sections of a black quilted fabric embedded into its surface, as if a jacket once covered the now mutilated body. Beasley's disarming combination of bright, fresh sneakers with the thick, fleshlike agglomeration creates a sense of rupture. The pose of the two sneakers underscores the work's evocation of violence and death. Whether housedresses, sneakers, or the many other items of clothing and things found in his artworks, Beasley's object choices establish strong connections to bodies, especially to black bodies, and to the social, political,

Untitled (Self-care product II), 2017. Resin, du-rags, and neckties. 63 x 45 x 4 inches (160.02 x 114.3 x 10.16 cm).

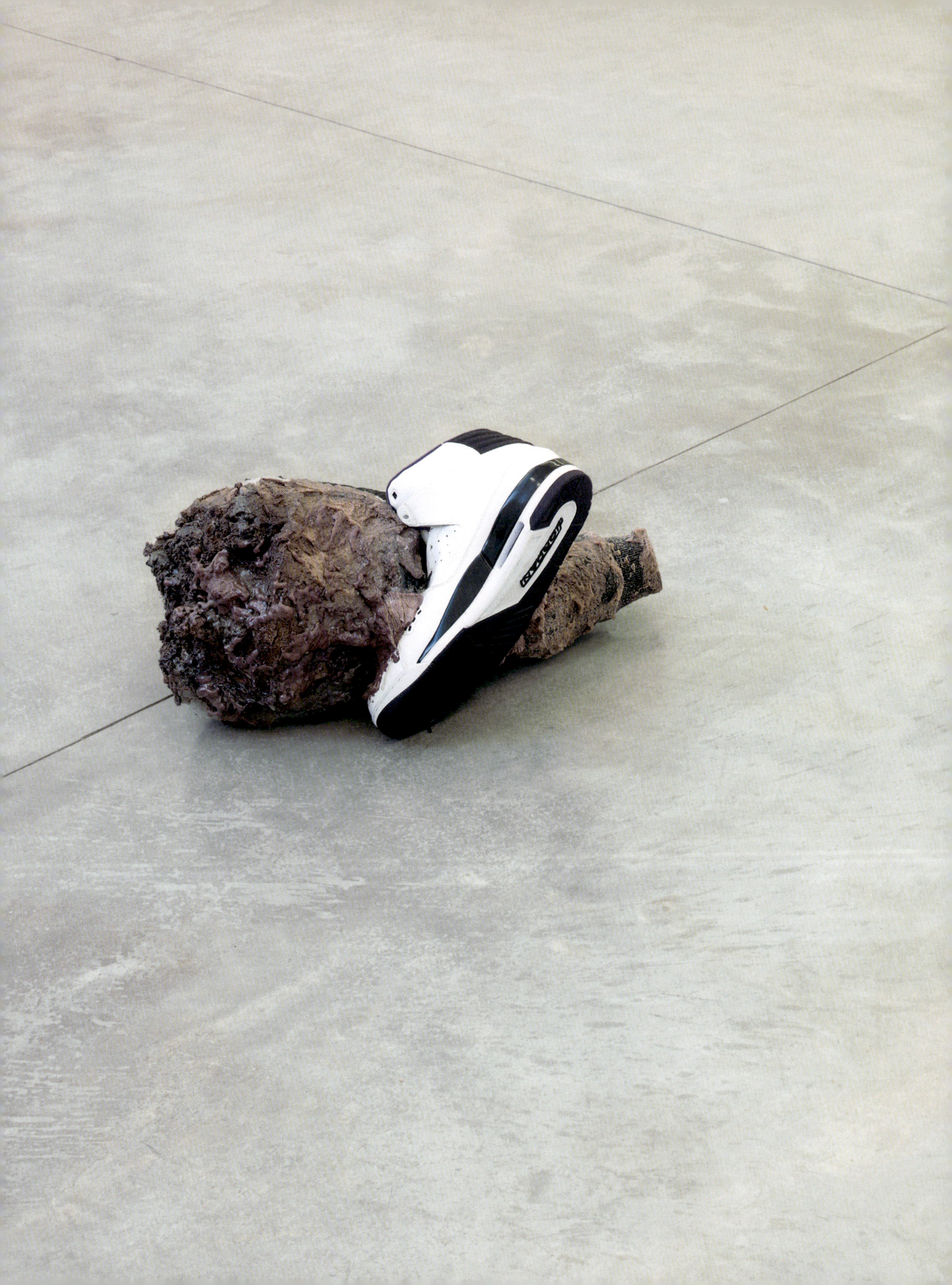

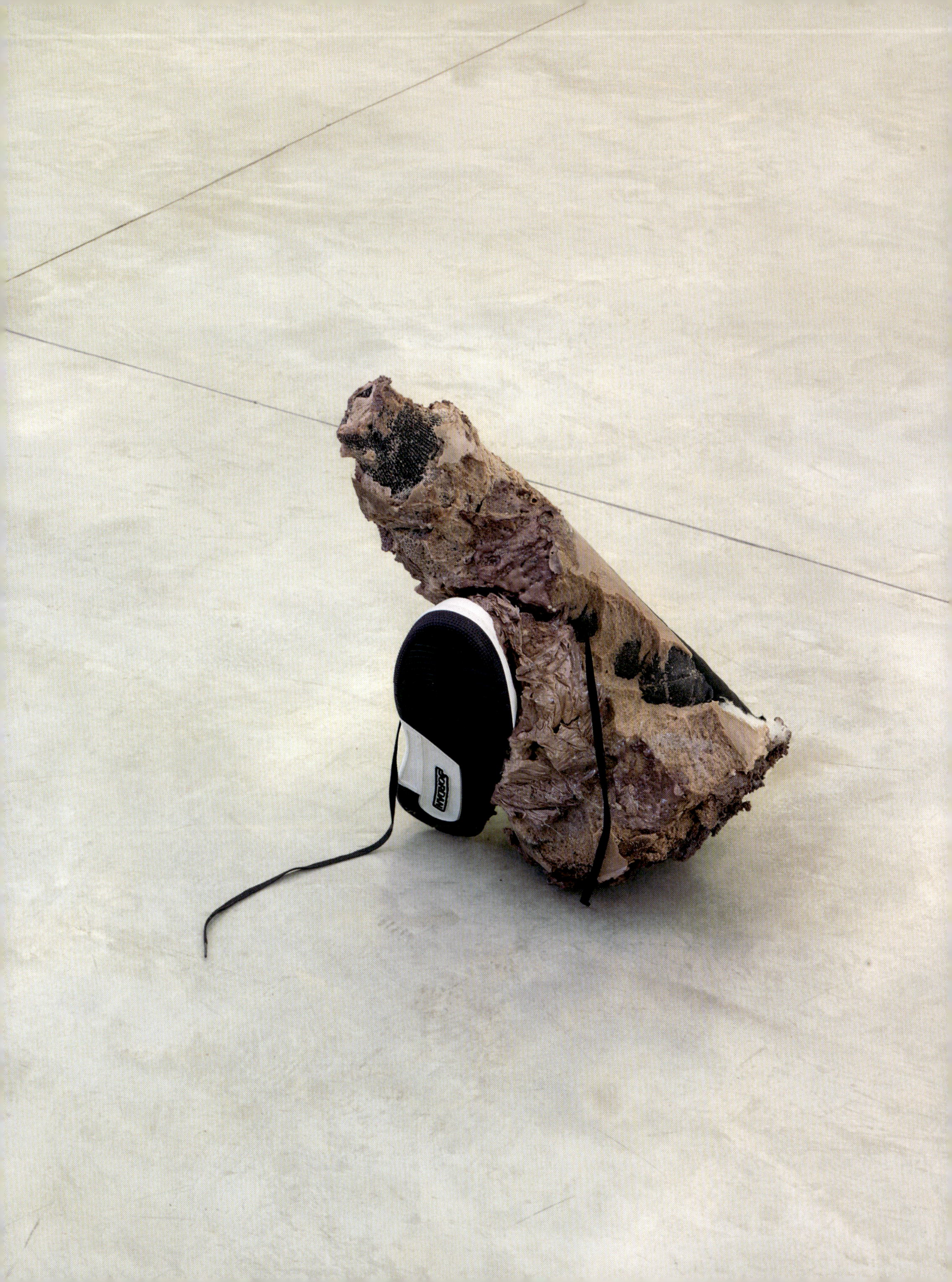

and cultural conditions that can make existence for those same bodies so difficult.

The subsequent stage of Beasley's process—his treatment of these objects—takes place in his studio or during performances, and his actions are as varied as his objects, but are often difficult for the viewer to ascertain by simply looking at or experiencing the final works. However, like the objects he chooses, his actions inflect his work with powerful social and ethical meanings. Many of the processes he employs have an alchemical quality: liquids set then fix to become solids, accidents and surprises abound, and empty areas or spaces become forms. Certainly Beasley develops these processes out of his desire for material to manifest itself and appear as he envisions, but it is also through these methods that he makes space aesthetically central to his work. And none of his artworks, even those that have no physical foot-print to speak of, would exist without physical—corporeal—space: that of skin, organs, and breath. He uses his own body in every process, hold-ing pieces in place as they set, pressing his knee or arm into the side of a sculpture, or drumming on the surfaces of his acoustic sculptures. By looking more closely at some of Beasley's recurrent actions in the studio and in performance, we can better understand how the artist connects bodies in space and the space of his body, and the ramifications of both.

Beasley began making space a central feature of his work by focus-ing on particular sites and indexing their historical, aural, or material residues. The artist's interest in site specificity can be traced back to the summer of 2011, between his first and second years of graduate school at Yale, while on a visit to his family's property in Virginia. It was the first time he had ever seen cotton plants flowering, and he was shocked to find out from his mother that the fields were planted with cotton. He made a number of photographs of the parcel and his family members on that trip. The pictures have an eerie quality: a man bends over in an expanse of water in *Drain* (2011–15) and a satellite dish appears to float against a screen of trees in *Untitled (Transmission)* (2011–15). The photographs juxtapose artifacts and people with places, yet the con-nections or relationships between these subjects and sites remain hazy, conjectural, abstract. If the blooming cotton field triggered in Beasley a reckoning with a site's relationship to slavery (my reading of his story), then this kind of abstraction is absolutely fundamental to the artist's documentation of the site. How else might we document—and trigger a reckoning with—something as horrific, as massive, and as unending as American slavery? Rather than the photographs being

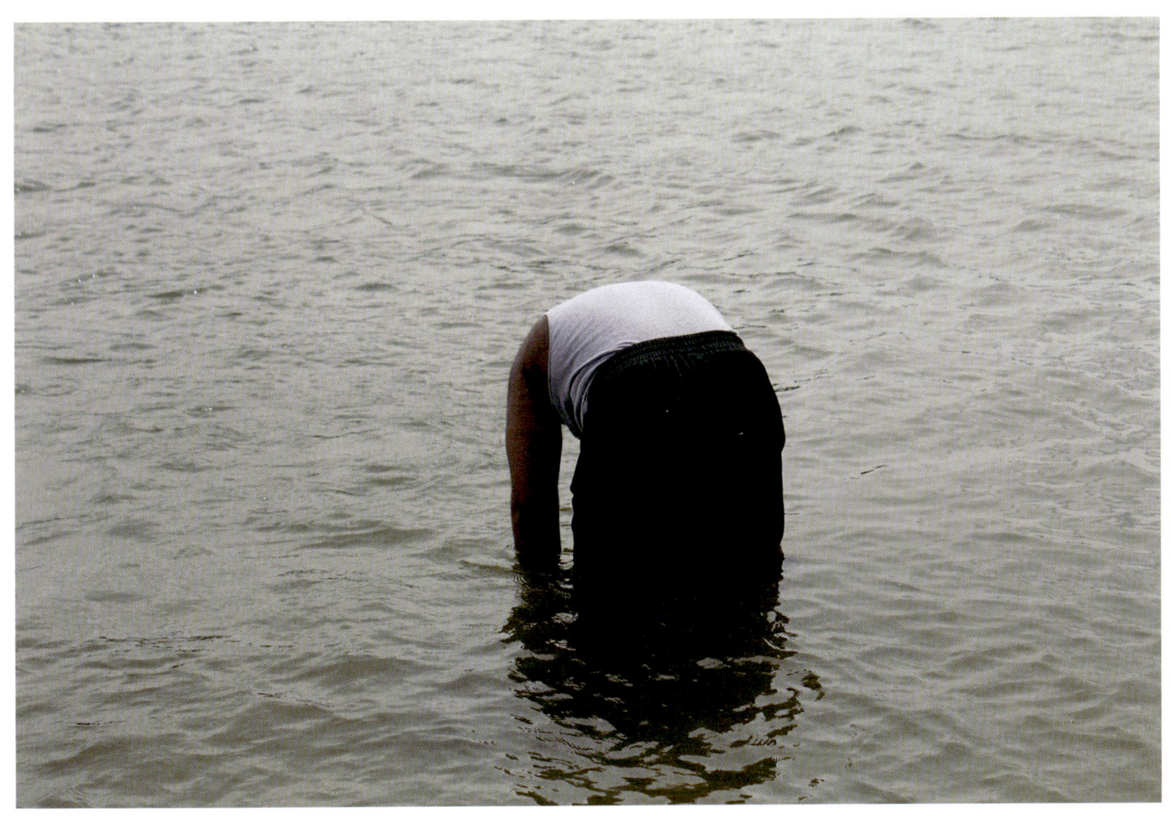

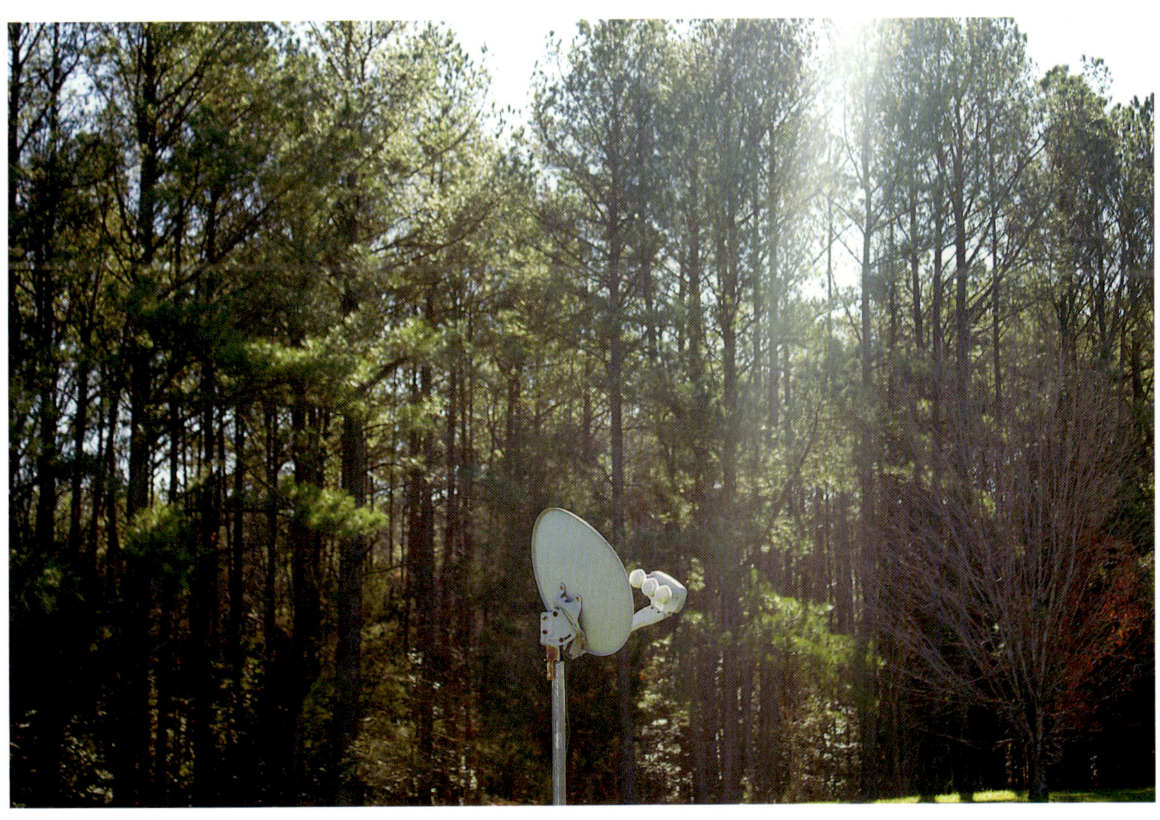

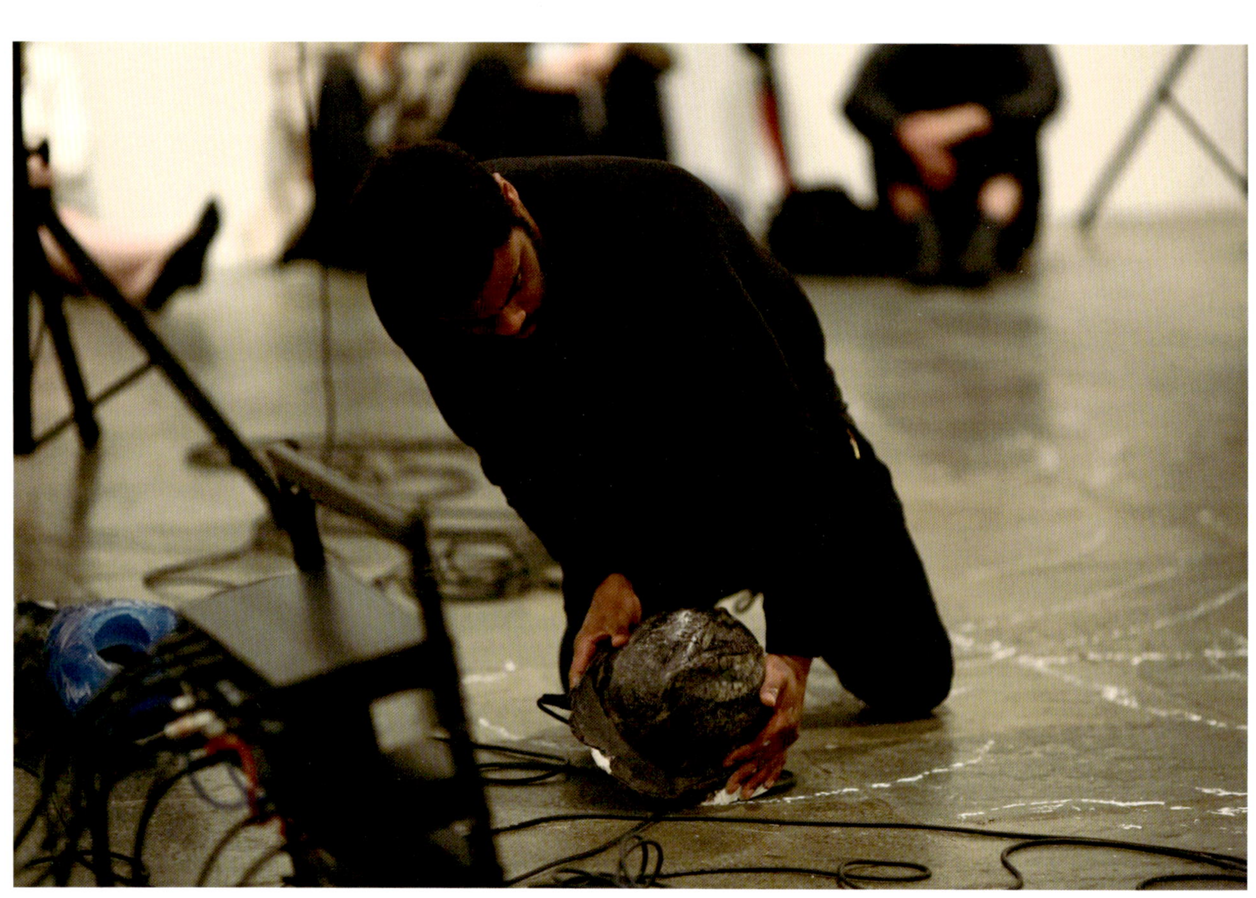

explicitly *about* slavery, I would suggest they reflect a pivotal moment in
which Beasley is exploring sites and their connections to collective and
personal histories and inventing new ways to give form to something
foreboding that is eternally present.

Over the next few years, Beasley undertook a series of field recordings, performances, and installations that harnessed site and sound as
material to pursue the dynamism of absence and presence. His performance *I Want My Spot Back*—first performed in the basement of the
sculpture department at Yale University, then at Saint Mark's Church in
New York City's East Village (a progressive Episcopal church known for
its long-standing tradition of presenting poetry and supporting social
justice activism and the arts), and finally, to wide acclaim, at the Museum
of Modern Art, New York, in 2012—consisted of thirty-nine slowed down
a cappella tracks by deceased black male rappers from the 1990s, the
decade of Beasley's youth.[6] Beasley's radical elongation transformed
the beats and rhymes into indecipherable and ghostly groans that projected from a bank of powerful speakers, and reverberated through the
audience members. For the duration of the performance, the mass of
the audience became a vessel through which disembodied voices of
dead rappers gained form, or "got their spot back."

Other performances took on site explicitly. The four-part performance *And in My Dream I Was Rolling on the Floor* (2014) took place in a
condemned mansion built in the 1850s by abolitionists in Cleveland. It
attuned listeners to the sounds of the building, which is believed to have
been a stop on the Underground Railroad, and conjured the bodies
that had moved through it.[7] In his work *As I rest under many skies, I hear
my body escape me* (2014), presented as part of the exhibition *When the
Stars Begin to Fall: Imagination and the American South* at the Studio
Museum in Harlem, Beasley played sounds recorded on his family's
Virginia property in the museum space, and in a set of headphones
played a recording he had made on-site at the museum, thus dislocating
site and sound as they are experienced by the visitor. His projects have
also brought him outdoors: *. . . all different: for I do, I suppose, partake of
multitude* (2013), a performance consisting of a live feed of thirty wind
chimes collected and installed by Beasley combined with prerecorded
sound bites, took place in a concrete lot in Brooklyn.[8] The project
description elaborates on Beasley's interest in the presence of a har-
monic multitude within the singularity of an initial note: "When one
strikes a bell there are several tones that prevail, yet the hum tone is one
that lies an octave below the strike tone, the resonance being that of

*Movement I: DEF/ACHE/
CRYSTALLINE/SLEEVE*,
2013–14. Performance view,
Whitney Biennial, Whitney
Museum of American Art, New
York, 2014. Courtesy Whitney
Museum of American Art, New
York. Photo by Paula Court.

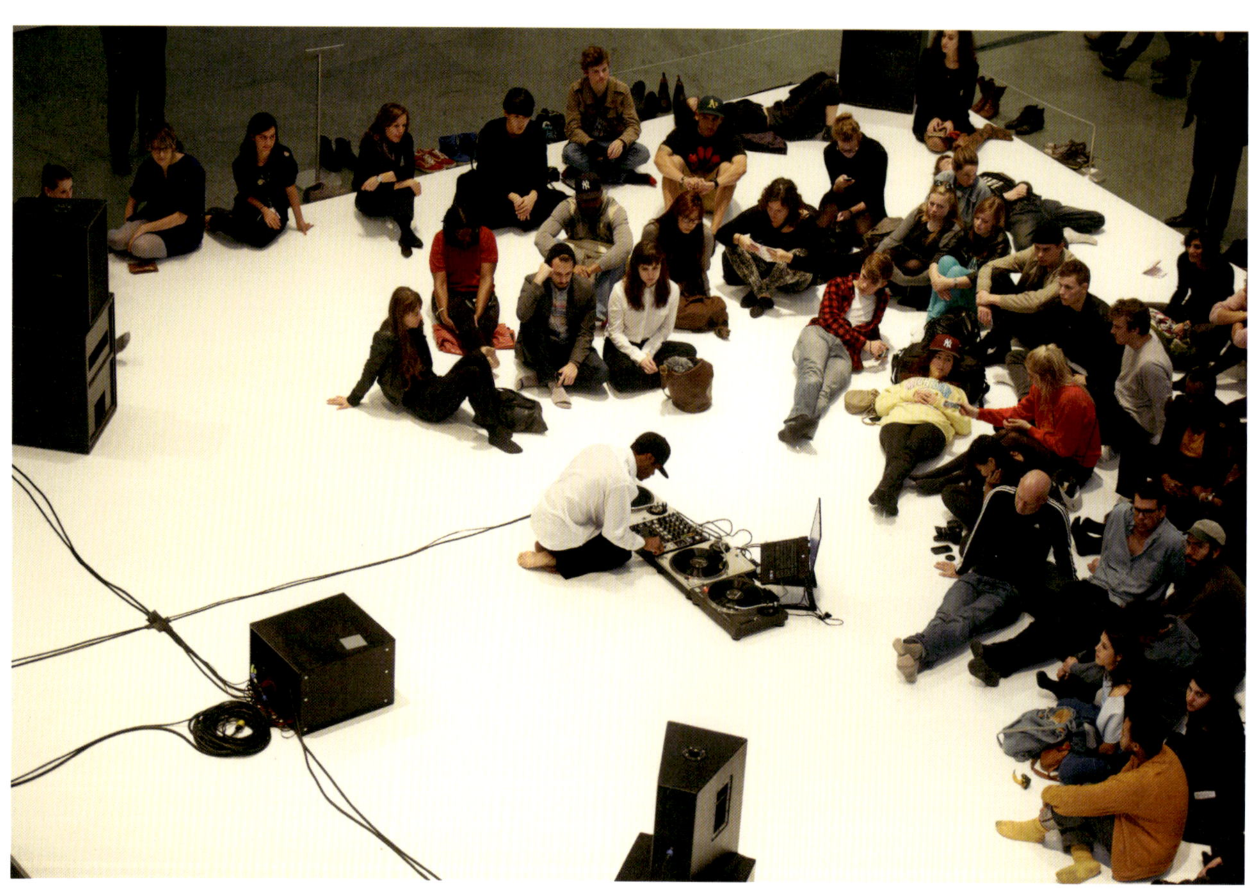

I Want My Spot Back, 2012.
Performance view, part of Ralph
Lemon's *Some Sweet Day*, Museum of
Modern Art, New York, 2012. Digital
image © The Museum of Modern Art/
Licensed by SCALA/Art Resource, NY.
Photo by Julia Cervantes.

Opposite top: *And in My Dream I Was
Rolling on the Floor*, 2014. Installation
view, Cozad-Bates House, Museum
of Contemporary Art, Cleveland,
curated by Rose Bouthillier, 2014.
Courtesy Museum of Contemporary Art,
Cleveland. Photo by Rose Bouthillier.

Opposite bottom: *. . . all different: for I
do, I suppose, partake of multitude*,
2013. Installation view, *6<<<>>>6
Part I*, Interstate Projects, Brooklyn, NY,
curated by Cleopatra's, 2013. Courtesy
the artist and Cleopatra's, Brooklyn,
New York. Photo by Marc Tatti.

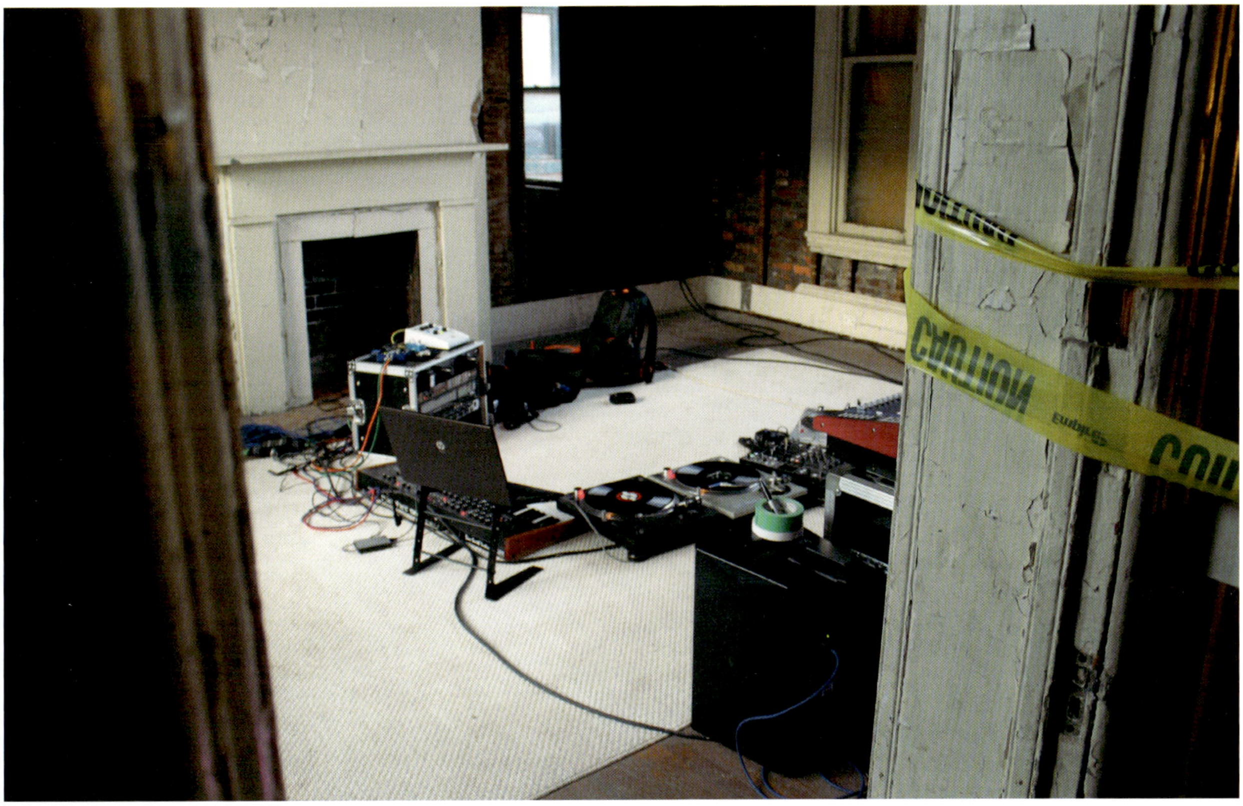

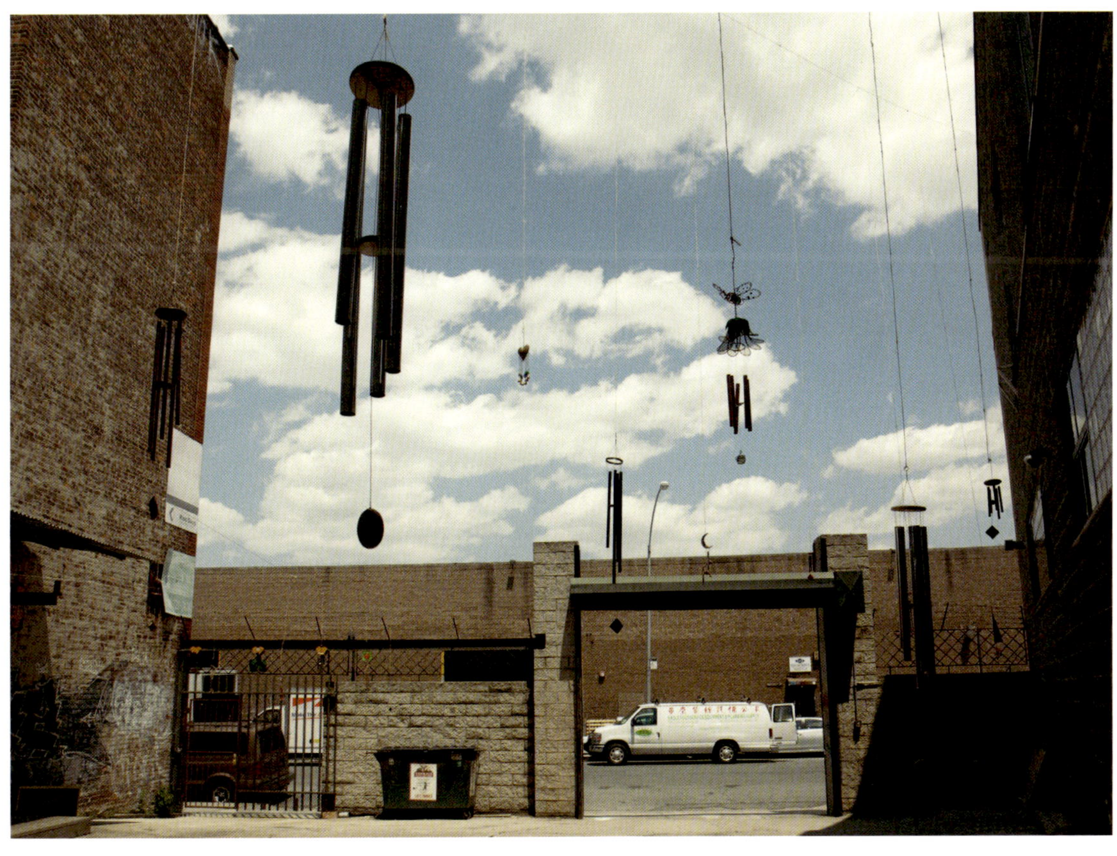

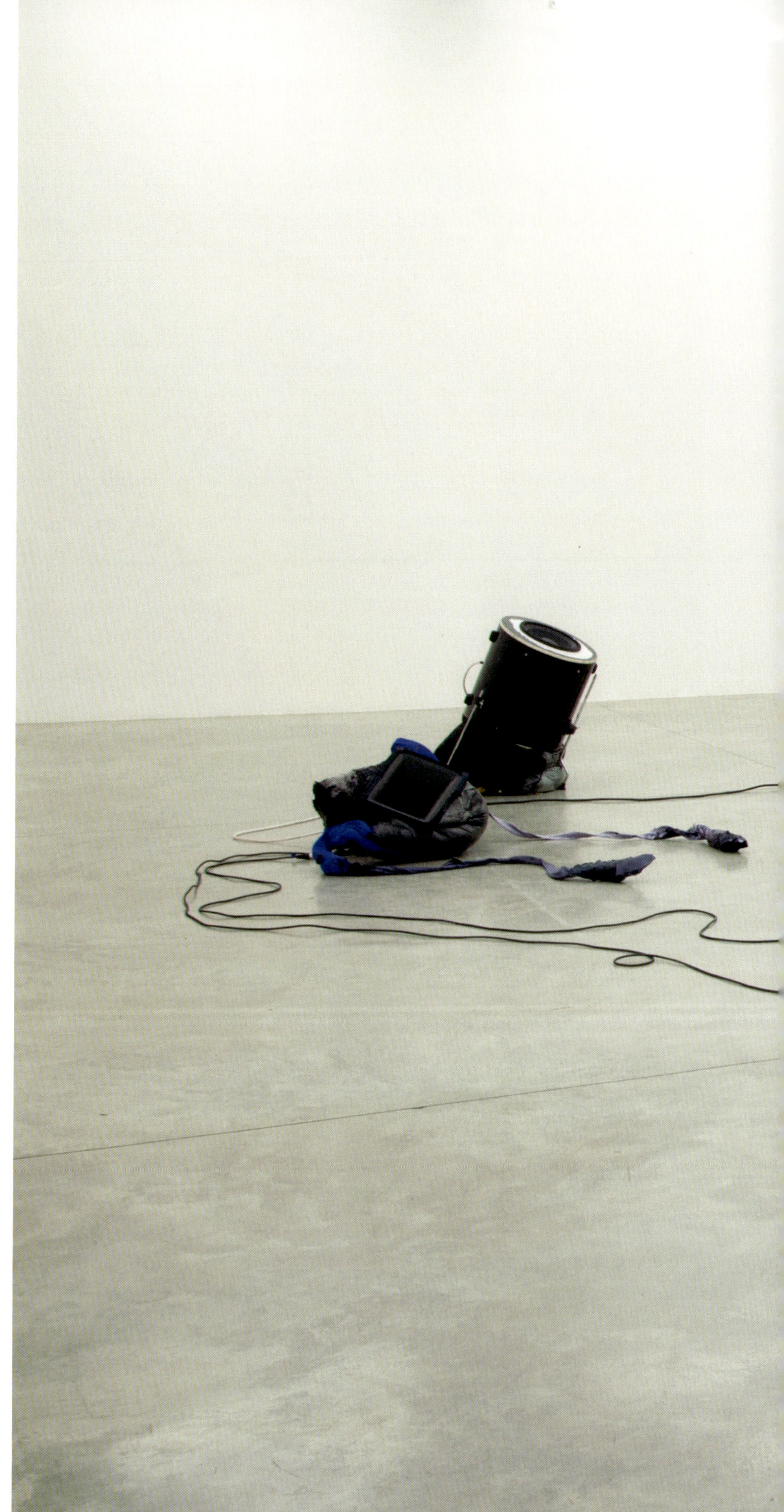

Movement II: BEATEN-FACE/ TOMS/ARMS, TIES, & LEG/ FLOOR/BODY/BASS, 2014. Resin, altered full-face respirator, panty hose, hypercardioid microphone, contact microphones, silicone, tom-tom drums, speaker drivers, audio components, polyurethane foam, neckties, dynamic micro-phones, floor tom, burned winter coat, bass drum, and power amp. Dimensions variable. Art Gallery of Ontario, Toronto.

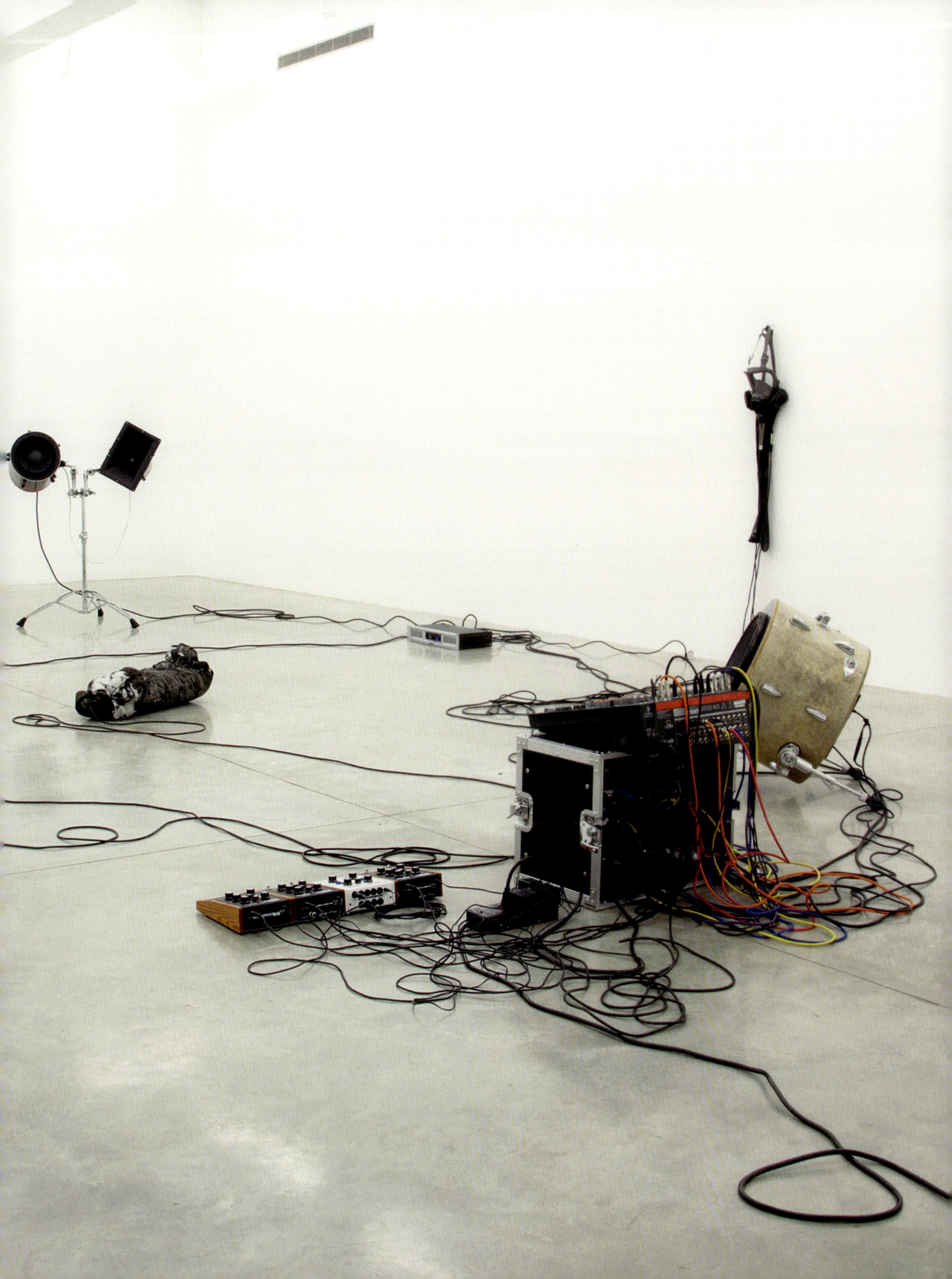

multiple tones within one note/or tone of an instrument. A layering
that happens at the time of the actual singular act where a multitude
is always produced. So what happens when 'we' recognize the initial
parts as a multitude and seek to expand that multitude exponentially?"[9]
In his performances and his series of sound-based sculptures and
installations, the artist explores myriad ways of embodying this multitude in order to render perceptible the multiplicity that exists in every
site, history, body, or sound but is frequently obscured in the moment
of creation and reception.

Beasley pursued these ideas and material reinventions in his sculpture practice as well, focusing on his studio and his own body. Near the
end of his yearlong residency at the Studio Museum in 2014, the artist
picked up the black shag rug that had been covering the floor of his
small studio in order to fix the marks of its, and his, occupancy. He had
paced the floor on this very same rug; it was where visitors had stood,
come and gone, and where the debris of his studio practice had fallen.
Retained within the swirling thick black fibers of this rug are chunks of
iridescent blue and remnants of colorful fabrics—the castoffs of his
sculptures and experiments. Beasley petrified all of this by pouring liquid
resin onto the rug and allowing it, within minutes, to fix the presence
of the past and the flux of his process. Wooden clothespins clipped to
the edges of the rug frame it as a composition, and five balls made
from his underwear and undershirts suspended by shoelaces dangle
against the conglomerate surface. This untitled work coalesces a number of experiments undertaken and strategies developed by Beasley
during his fruitful residency—an opportunity that inspired him to quit his
day job and fully dedicate himself to his art.[10] This integration of his own
clothing and the physicality of his manipulations endowed his early
sculptures with an anthropomorphic quality, producing a kind of surro-
gacy: his works began to stand in for bodies, or parts of bodies. The
substitution is emphatic in sculptures like *Untitled (Chest Pack)* and
Untitled (Chest Compression) (both 2014), where automotive jumper
cables and a shop vacuum dressed in clothing call to mind the heart and
lung of the human body while underscoring the circulation of blood, air,
and electrical charge.

Beasley's suspended sculptures *Strange Fruit (Pair 1)* and *(Pair 2)*
(both 2015), made for the Solomon R. Guggenheim Museum's *Storylines*
exhibition, deftly braid together his various sculpture-making and
performance strategies. Intended to be handled and activated during
impromptu performances, these sculptures—made from sneakers

Untitled, 2014. Shag rug,
polyurethane foam, resin,
clothespins, thermal shirts,
underwear, and studio debris.
80 x 50 x 5 inches (203.2 x 127 x
12.7 cm). Collection of
Lonti Ebers, New York.

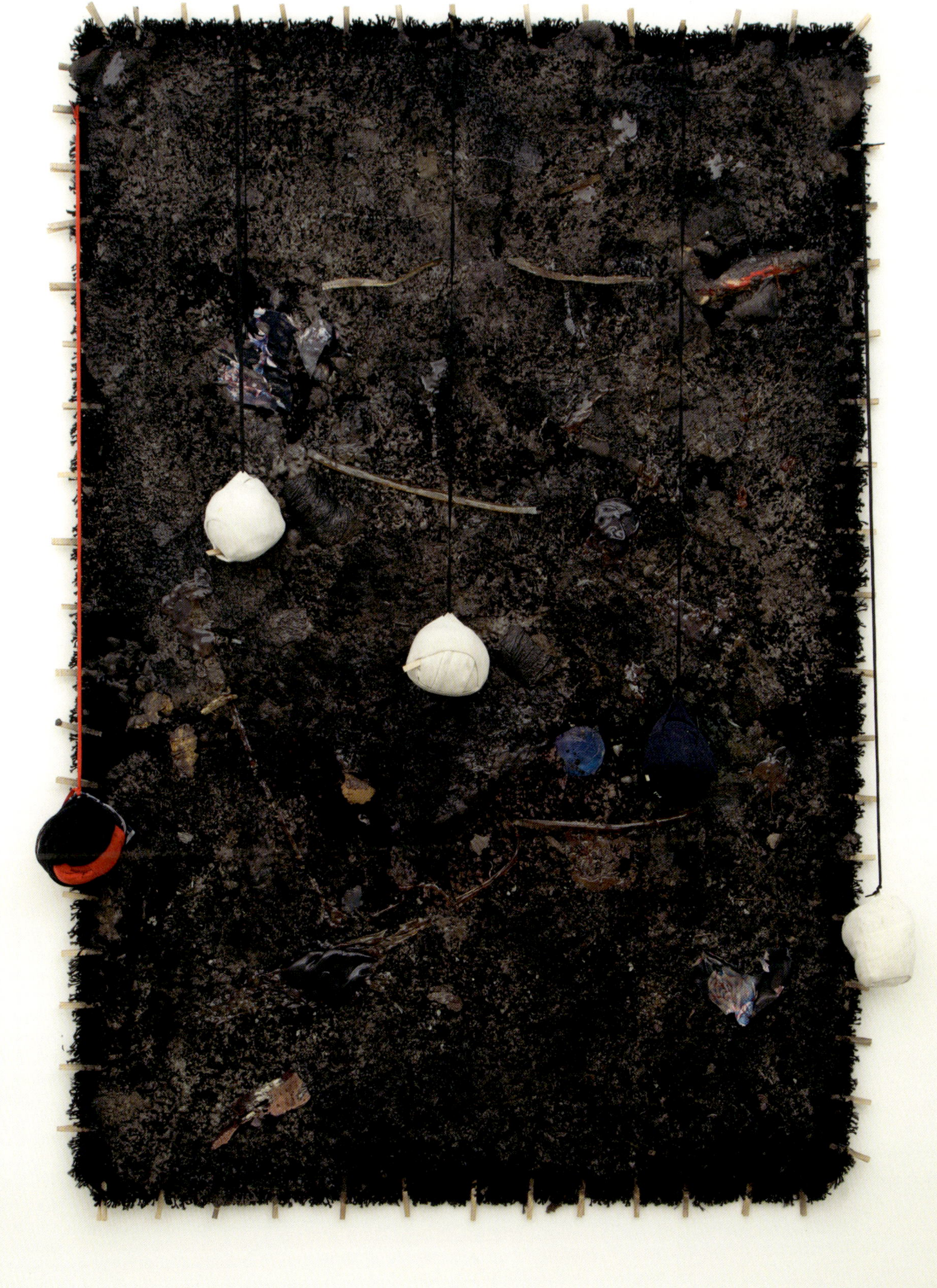

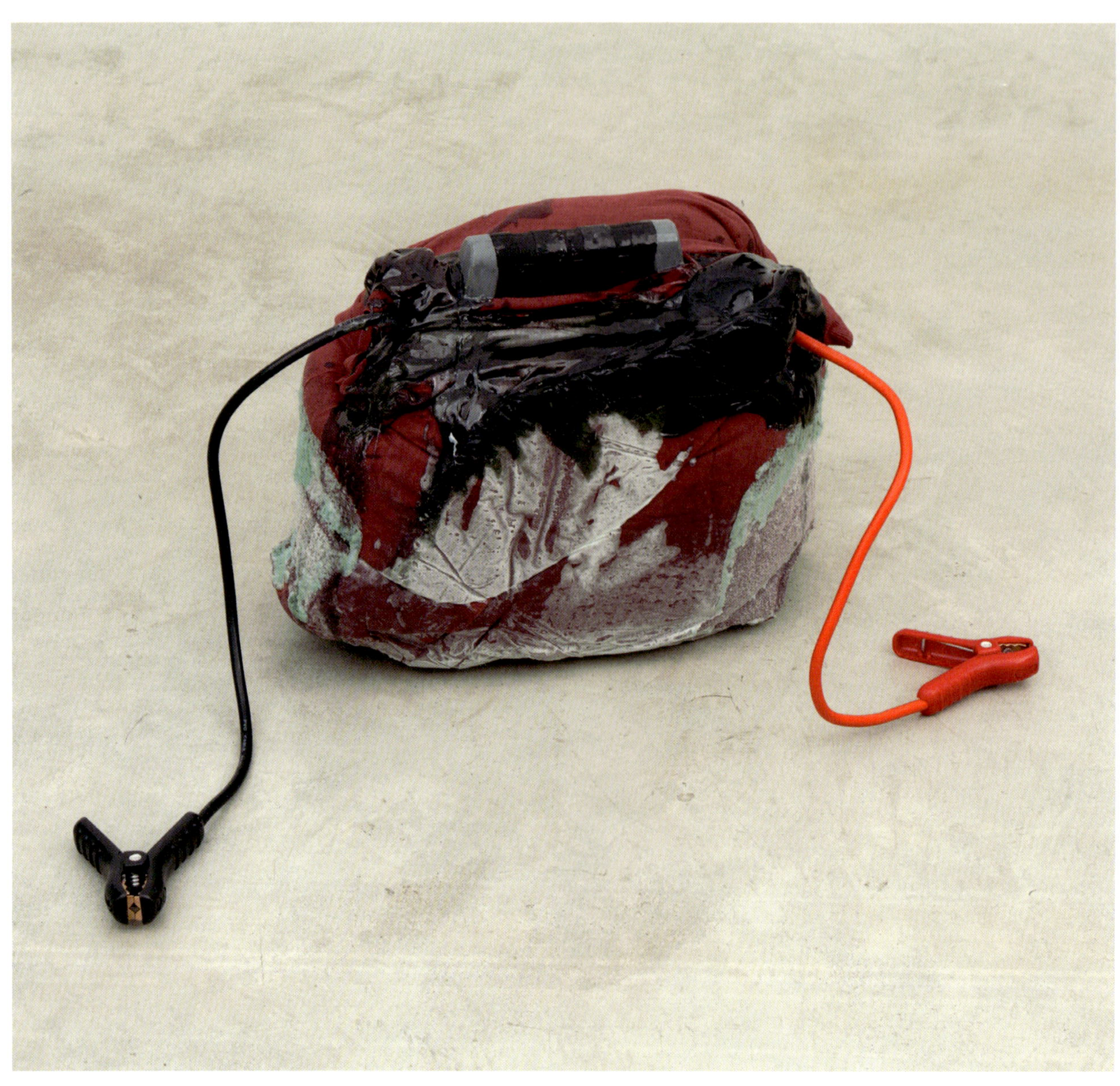

Untitled (chest pack), 2014. Urethane foam, resin, long-sleeve shirt, and battery charger. 13½ x 30 x 12 inches (34.3 x 76.2 x 30.5 cm). Collection of Martin and Rebecca Eisenberg, Scarsdale, NY.

Opposite: *Untitled (chest compression)*, 2014. Air compressor, resin, polyurethane foam, and Peter Max signature reversible long-sleeve shirt. 23½ x 19 x 17 inches (59.7 x 48.3 x 43.2 cm). Rennie Collection, Vancouver, BC.

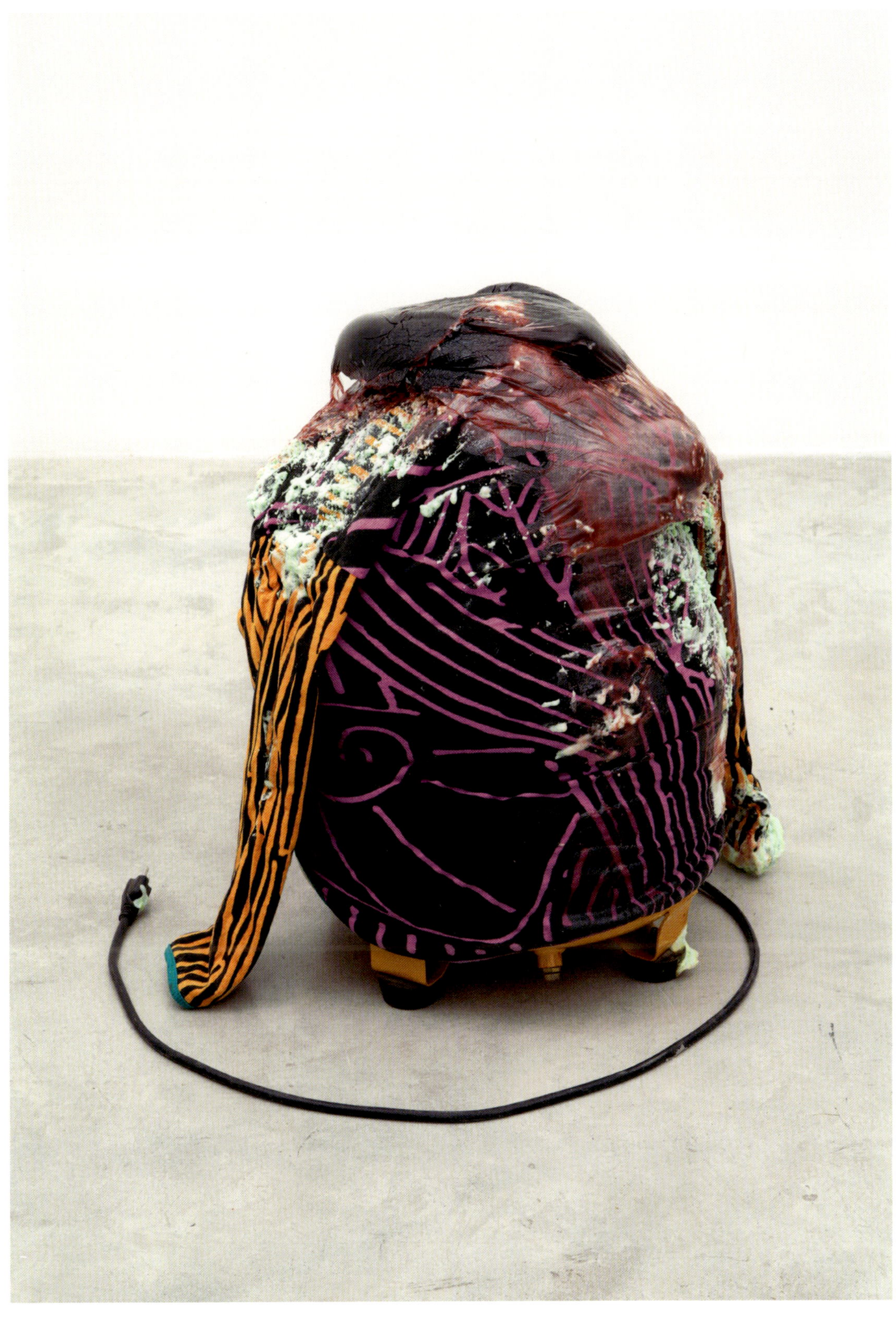

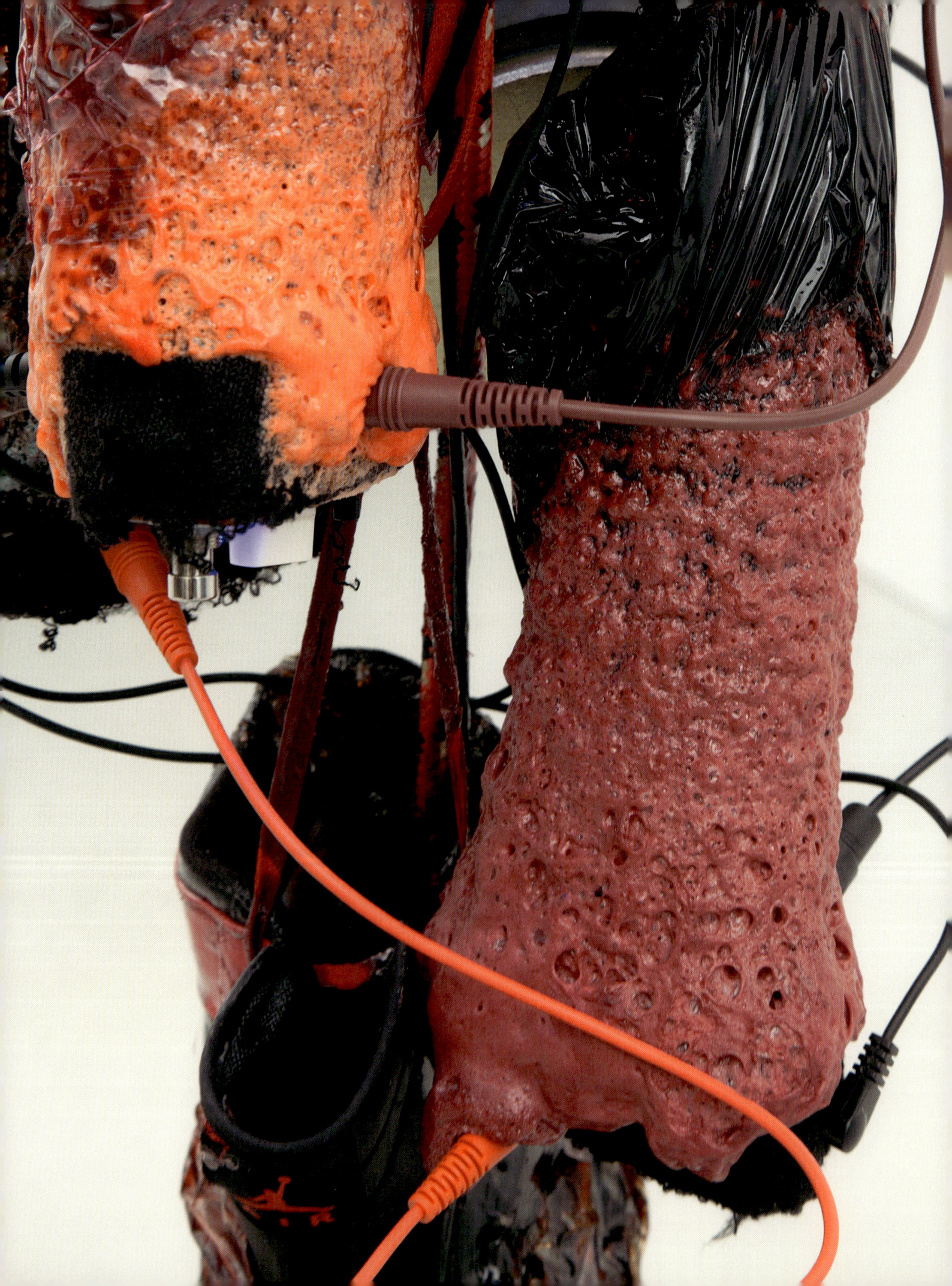

Opposite: *Strange Fruit (Pair 2)* (detail), 2015. Nike Air Jordan 1 shoes (red and black), resin, polyurethane foam, tube socks, shoelaces, rope, speakers, hypercardioid and contact microphones, amplifiers, patch cables, and effects processors. 66 x 24 x 20 inches (167.6 x 61 x 50.8 cm). Collection of Lonti Ebers, New York.

Strange Fruit (Pair 1), 2015. Nike Air Jordan 1 shoes (white and black), resin, polyurethane foam, tube socks, shoelaces, rope, speakers, hypercardioid and contact microphones, amplifier, patch cables, and effects processors. Dimensions variable. Solomon R. Guggenheim Museum, New York. Commissioned by the Young Collectors Council with additional funds contributed by Josh Elkes, Younghee Kim-Wait, and Julia and Jamal Nusseibeh, 2014. 2014.74.

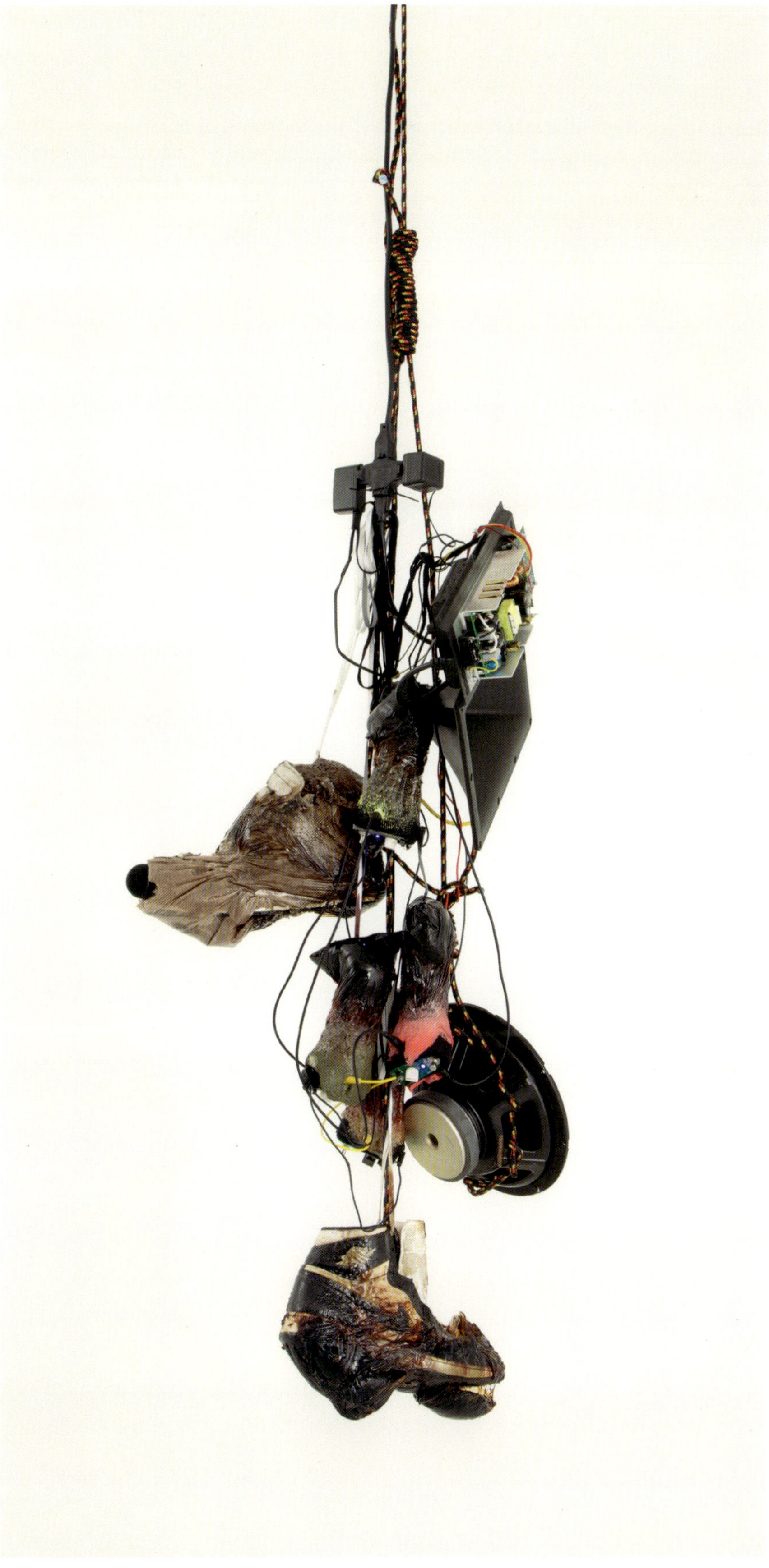

embedded with mics and speakers and other electronic musical equipment hanging from wires—absorb and reflect the sounds of the space: the voices of onlookers, the breath of the performer, and the drone of the building's mechanical equipment. Beasley's use of "Strange Fruit" as the work's title (after the legendary song written by Bronx schoolteacher Abel Meeropol in 1937, and famously performed and recorded by Billie Holiday and Nina Simone, and even sampled by Kanye West) deepens the work's reference to lynched black bodies. "Southern trees bear strange fruit / (Blood on the leaves, blood at the root)," Meeropol's song begins. More than the title or the sneakers, however, it is the purples, reds, and oranges; the textures like pores and blistered skin; and the bulges that bring to mind violated bodies and that guide us toward seeing bodies in what we obviously can identify as commonplace stuff one buys with a quick online click, or at brick-and-mortar stores such as Foot Locker or RadioShack. In the moment of performance, might the sculpture and the performers summon the spectral bodies of some 5,000-recorded lynchings through the space and bodies of the museum?[11] This would not be an emancipatory move, a suture, a belonging, but rather a means to, quoting Christina Sharpe, "depict aesthetically the impossibility of such resolutions by representing the paradoxes of blackness within and after the legacies of slavery's denial of Black humanity." Sharpe continues, "I name this paradox the wake, and I use the wake in all of its meanings as a means of understanding how slavery's violences emerge within the contemporary conditions of spatial, legal, psychic, material, and other dimensions of Black non/being as well as in Black modes of resistance."[12] *Strange Fruit* circulates in the paradox of presence/absence (or being/nonbeing), unveiling the multitudes of every crevice, cord, voice, and second. This happens on the most literal level as one's eyes run across the heavily worked surfaces, reveling in their textures and details, which appear to obscure as much as to delineate the forms that lie beneath, just out of sight.

Industrial materials, especially liquid polyurethane resin, expand Beasley's ability to fix flexible materials and to capture indeterminate physical states. The alchemy of turning liquid into a solid while retaining the sense of a morphing state vastly expanded Beasley's formal vocabulary. It also posed new challenges, especially given the short hardening time of resin. The artist invented novel support structures in order to manage the hardening process of the resin and the various forms the material would take. Repurposed objects such as mic stands and Styrofoam mannequin heads served as molds and casts to fix his

Movement III (Karaoke), 2014. Bass drum shells, polyurethane foam, resin, T-shirts, subwoofer driver, amplifier, contact microphones, Shure SM58 microphone, and audio equipment. Two parts: first part, 60 x 36 x 48 inches (152.4 x 91.4 x 121.9 cm); second part, 29½ x 15 x 19 inches (74.9 x 38.1 x 48.3 cm). Richard Chang Collection, New York.

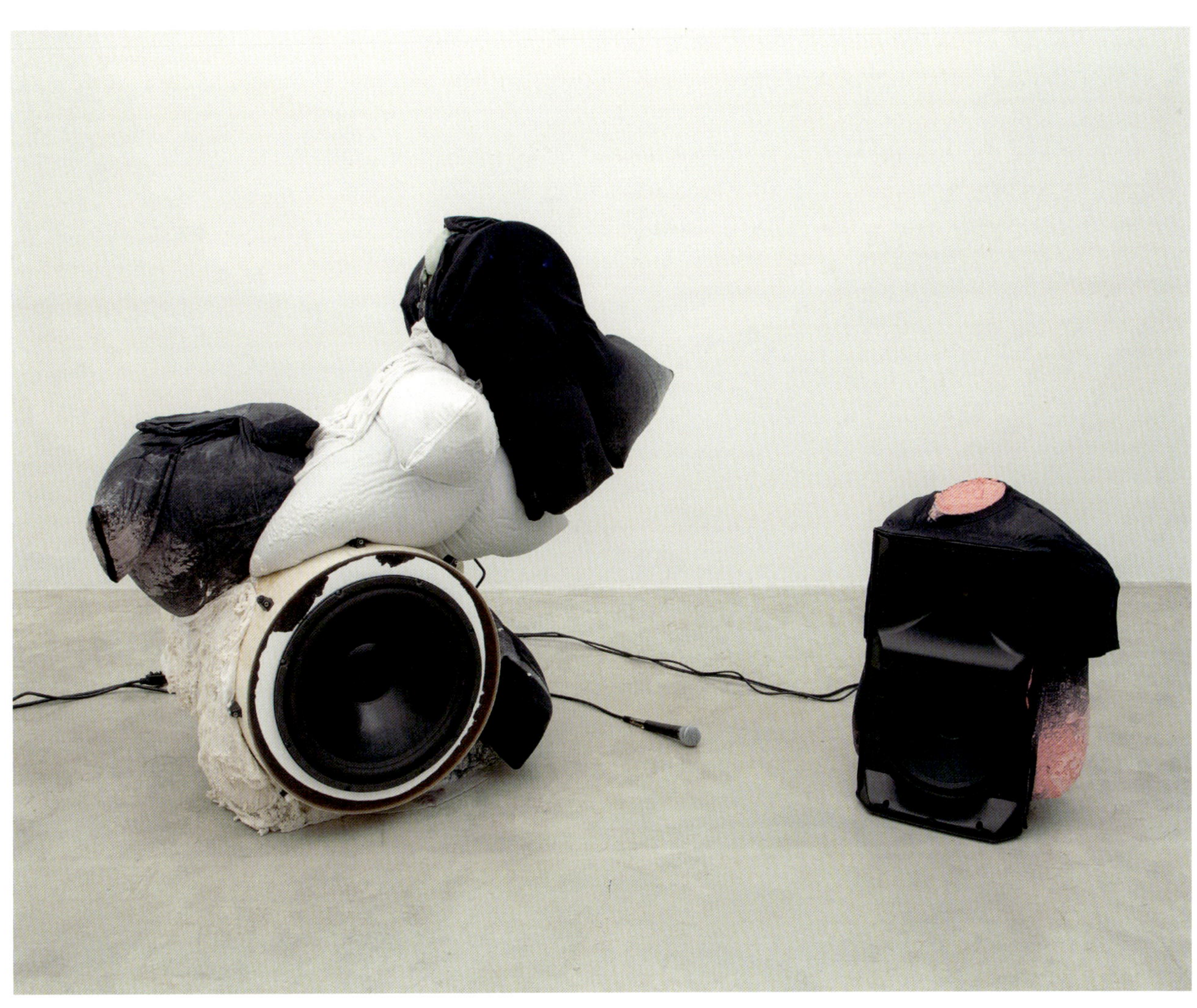

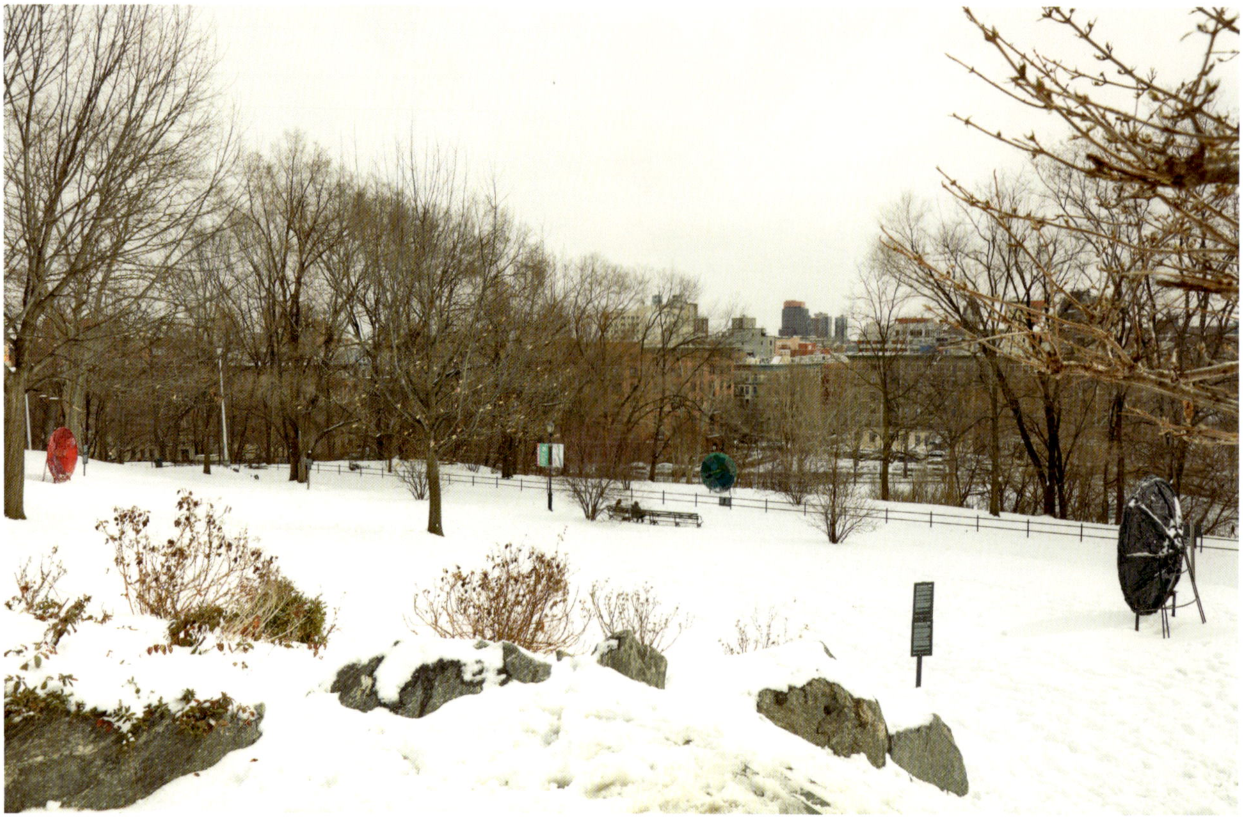

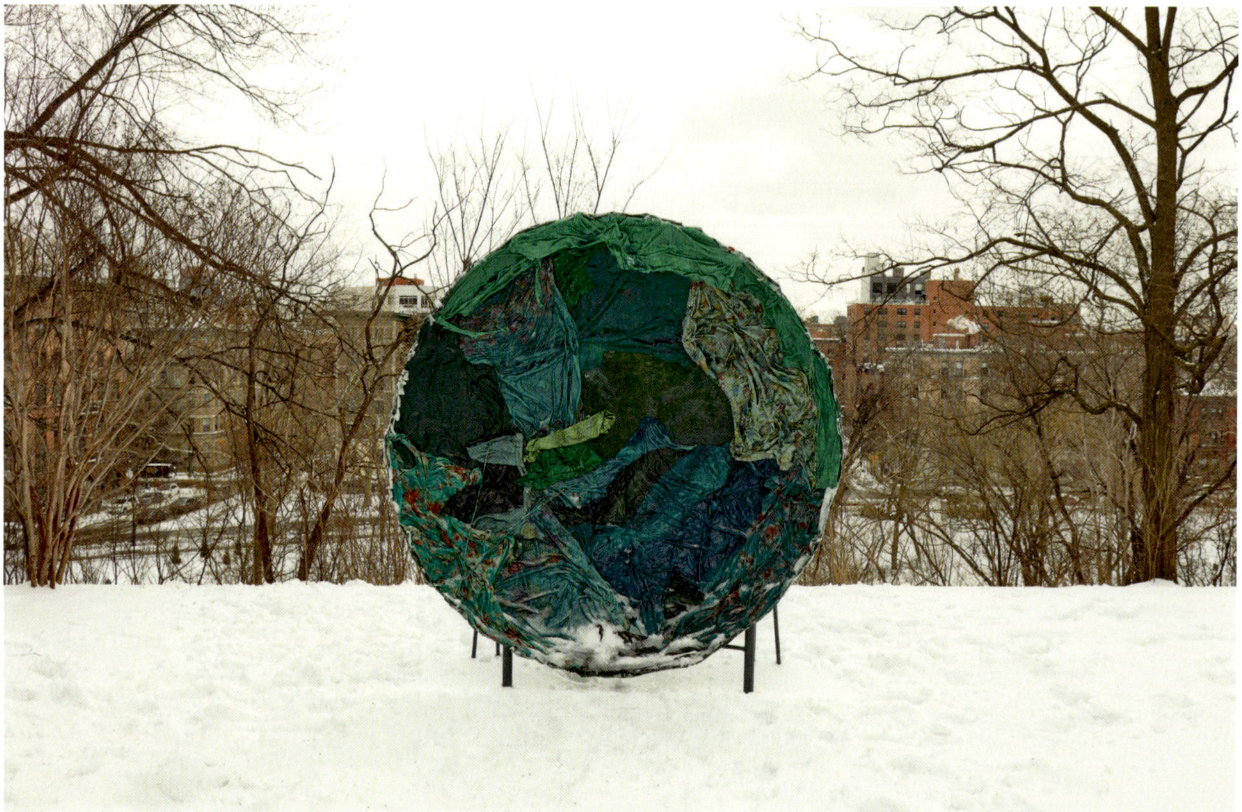

resin-dipped clothing into diverse shapes that attached to the wall or stood on the floor. His work tended to evolve serially, each new form engaged with the dynamic of absence/presence, generating potent metaphors of, and relationships to, bodily experience.

For his series of "acoustic mirror" sculptures, Beasley employed the form of the satellite dish—invented to aggregate diverse signals—to make concave sculptures that can hinge off the wall on TV mounts or stand freely. He forms these sculptures by layering clothing into the cavity of a parabolic or dish-shaped mold, pouring resin over it, and allowing it to set. Within the overall disc shape, hundreds of minute manipulations are made to the clothing, which articulate the surfaces of the sculptures. The poetics of generation inherent to the casting and creative process mirror the operations of the dish, which concentrates sound or radio waves via reflection to a focal point in order to produce a powerful wave that can be directed and transmitted. Out of the inchoate and unorganized noise emerges a power, a positive, a form, a body. By enabling his acoustic mirror sculptures to be angled in relation to the plane of the wall, Beasley connects his sculptures to the particularities of the space—its architecture, materials, and containment of bodies—which he was simultaneously pursuing in his performances. A viewer standing in front of *Untitled (11)* (2015) might recognize herself in the familiar items, such as hats, T-shirts, and pillowcases, flattened and melted into the concave form, and also in the activity of projecting and receiving sound, her body organized via the sculpture's mirroring and consolidation of sound waves. The often-untitled "acoustic mirror" sculptures furnish what could be described as a "projected body" that includes artifacts of multiple bodies as well as the sonic environment and built space.

As if seeking to further summon the body, in 2015 Beasley began laying resin-impregnated clothing over Styrofoam mannequin heads and rounded forms supported by microphone stands to create "ghosts." In these works, the void becomes a primary subject, as jackets, housedresses, and T-shirts fashion the contours of bodies, but faces remain blank. In *Untitled (. . . just watch)* (2015), a Nautica rain jacket stands on the floor. Its hood appears filled, as if covering a person's head, and then the shoulders fall away. The body and arms are either absent or too small to fill the raincoat. The jacket, which was Beasley's in high school, appears to deflate from top to bottom. The sculpture is roughly the height of a child, coming up to the waist of an adult viewer standing before it. The shrouded face and apparent exhaustion of breath below

Top: *Who's Afraid to Listen to Red, Black and Green?*, 2016. Installation view, Morningside Park, New York, 2016–17. From *inHarlem: Kevin Beasley*, The Studio Museum in Harlem, New York. Photo by Jason Wyche.

Bottom: *Who's Afraid to Listen to Red, Black and Green?* (detail), 2016. Installation view, Morningside Park, New York, 2016–17. From *inHarlem: Kevin Beasley*, The Studio Museum in Harlem. Photo by Jason Wyche.

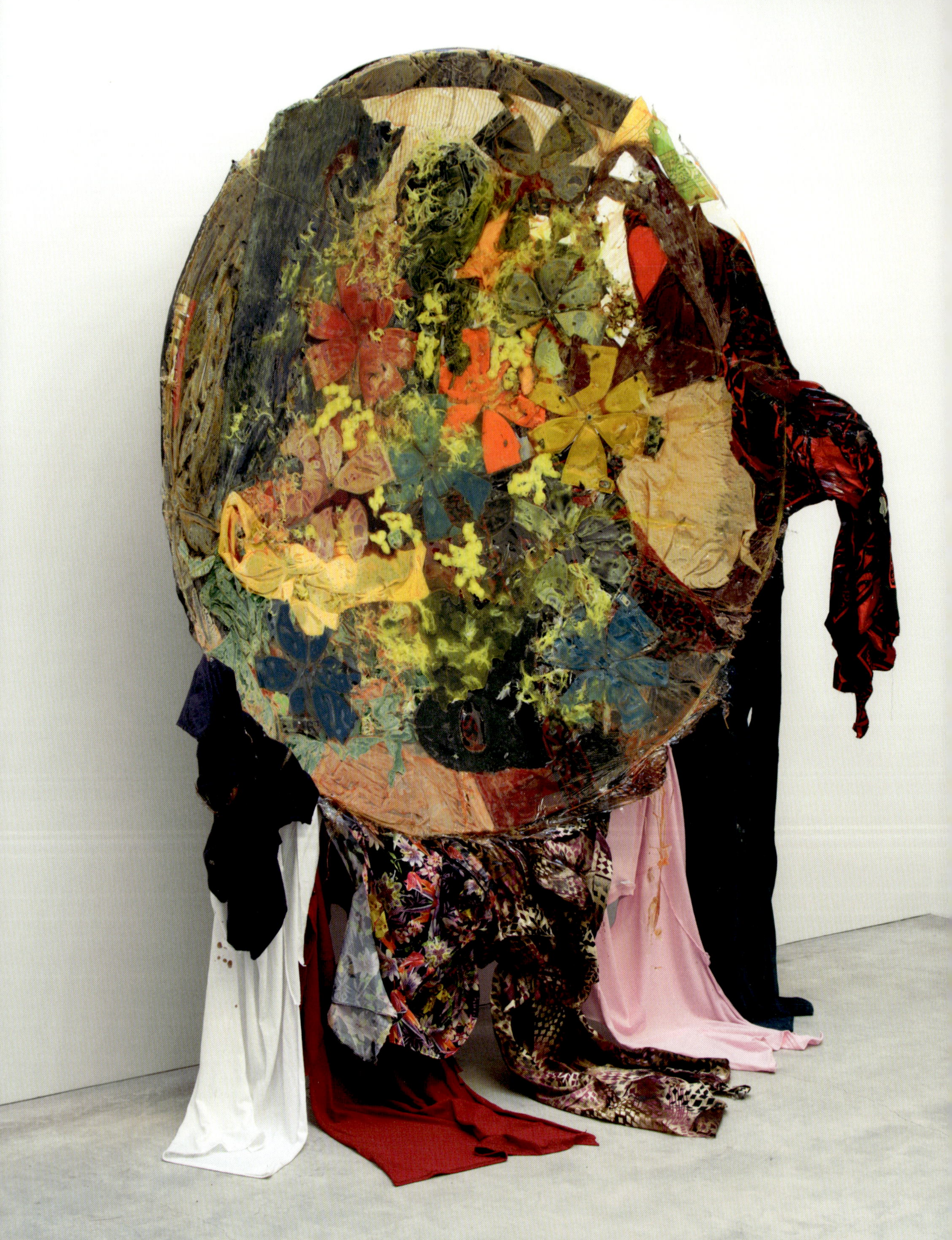

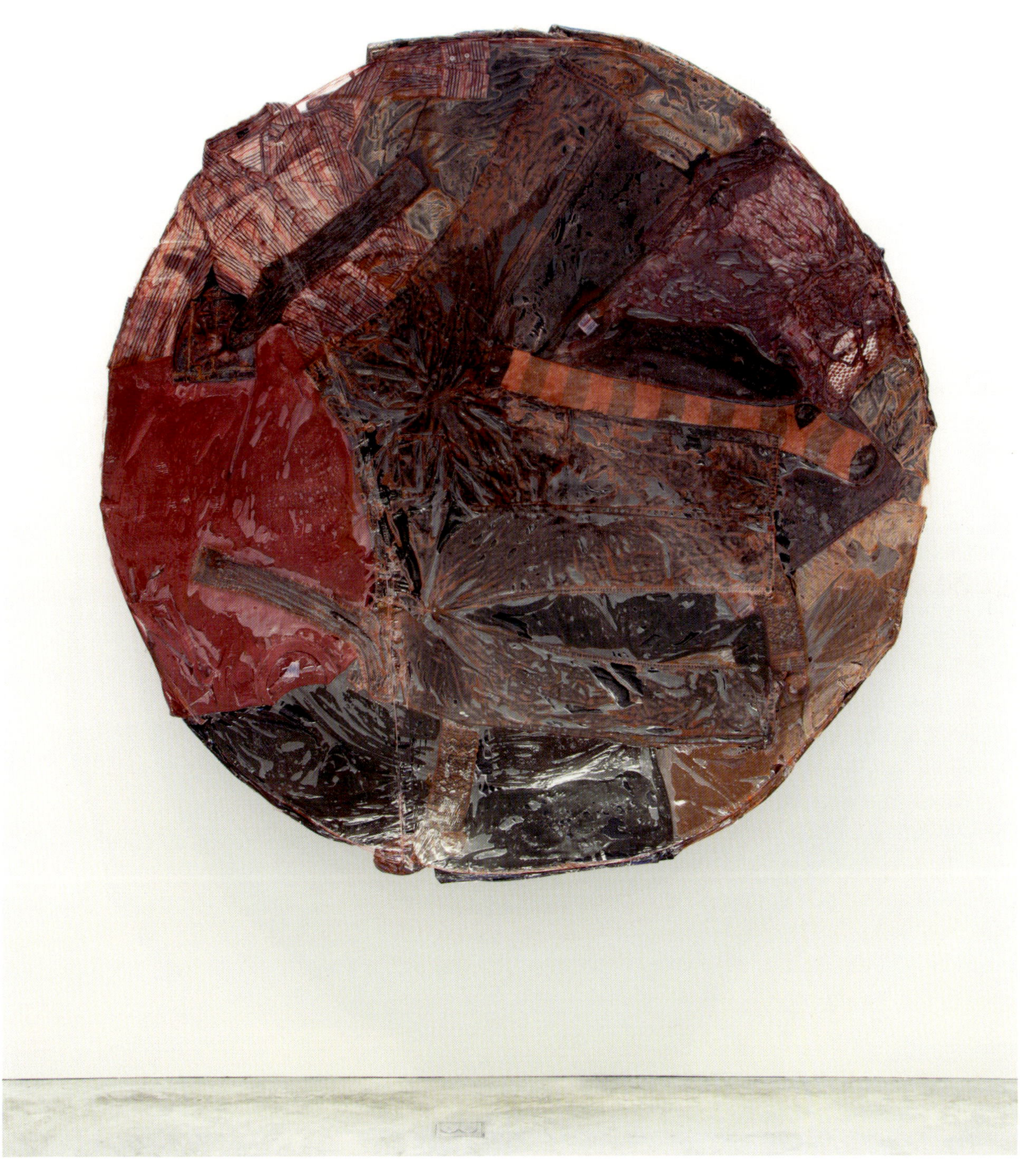

Opposite: *Untitled (11)*, 2015. Altered New Era fitted hats, housedresses, T-shirts, bandanas, studio debris, pillowcases, resin, down feathers, raw cotton, and television mount. 94 x 77 x 28 inches (238.8 x 195.6 x 71.1 cm). Rennie Collection, Vancouver, BC.

Untitled, 2015. Collared shirts, T-shirts, socks, pants, television mount, and resin. 70 x 70 x 16 inches (177.8 x 177.8 x 40.6 cm). Private collection, New York.

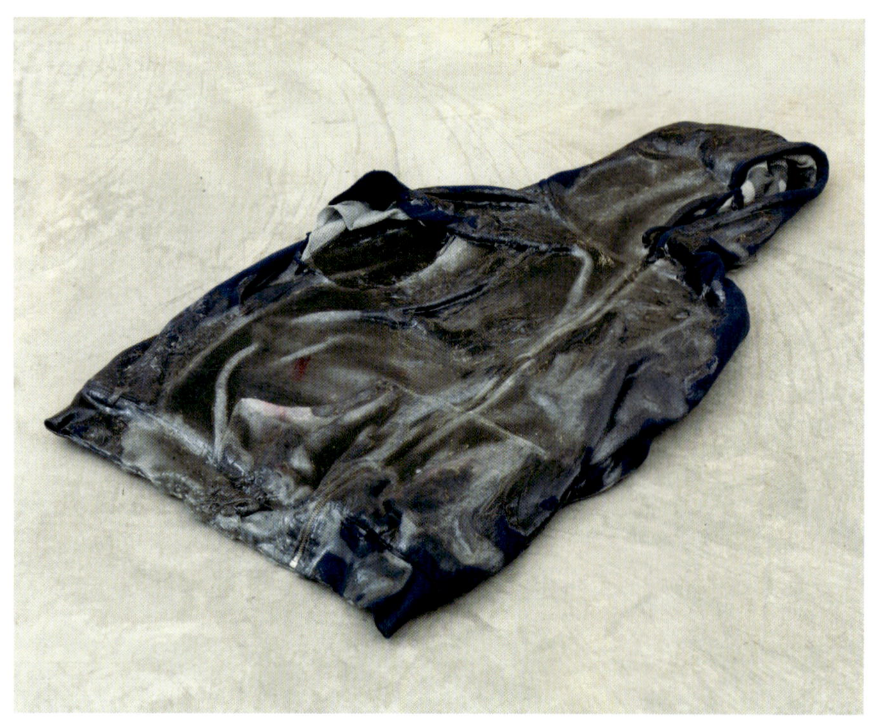

... *ain't it?*, 2014. Hooded
sweatshirt and resin. 21 x 37 x
2½ inches (53.3 x 94 x 6.4 cm).
Rennie Collection, Vancouver, BC.

the neck elicits a sense of death, of life squeezed out; the bottom of the
jacket pools lifelessly on the floor.

Beasley made this work in 2015, the same year NYPD officer
Daniel Pantaleo was acquitted in the murder of Eric Garner, who died
on July 17, 2014, from, according to the medical examiner's report,
compression of the neck and chest; the same year Cleveland police
gunned down twelve-year-old Tamir Rice on a playground; and three
years after George Zimmerman murdered Trayvon Martin, citing the
boy's "dark hoodie" as suspect.[13] Garner's final pleas for his life—"I can't
breathe, I can't breathe . . ." (eleven times)—while trapped in Pantaleo's
chokehold, became a cry of outrage against these and many other
instances of police brutality and murder, while the hoodie rose to become
a widely recognized symbol of resistance.[14] Beasley's sculpture is not
a response to any one instance of murder or brutality but rather an evocation of a bodily state, a passing in plain sight. The work's title, *just
watch*, could be read as a call to witness. Perhaps we are called out of
resignation to the inevitable: "Just watch." Perhaps this is an instruction
to watch our backs. Or maybe this is a pointedly taunting response to
our utter disbelief.

Opposite: *Untitled (. . . just watch)*,
2015. Nautica rain jacket and
resin. 37 x 38 x 20 inches
(94 x 96.5 x 50.8 cm). Collection
of Brian McMahon, New York.

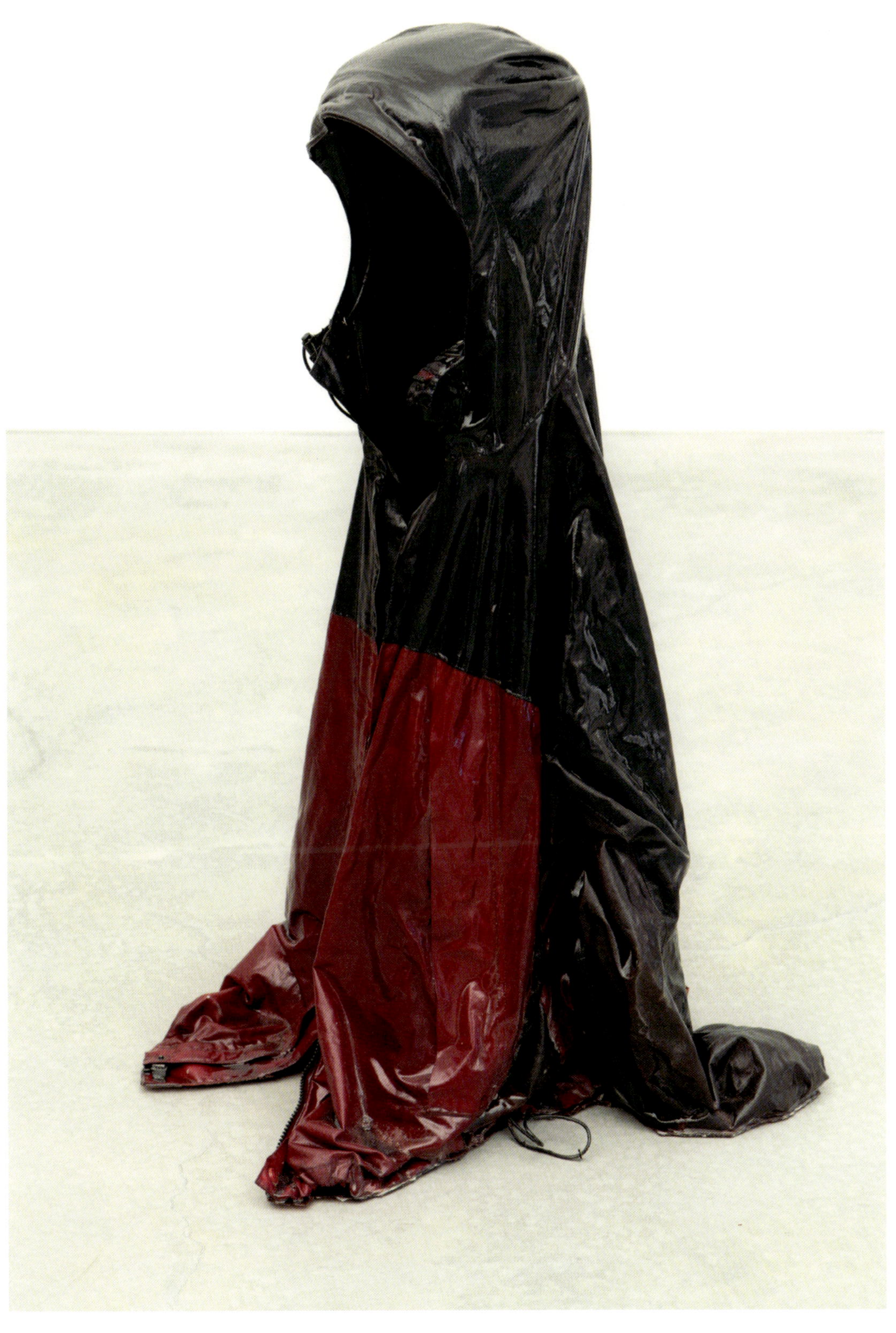

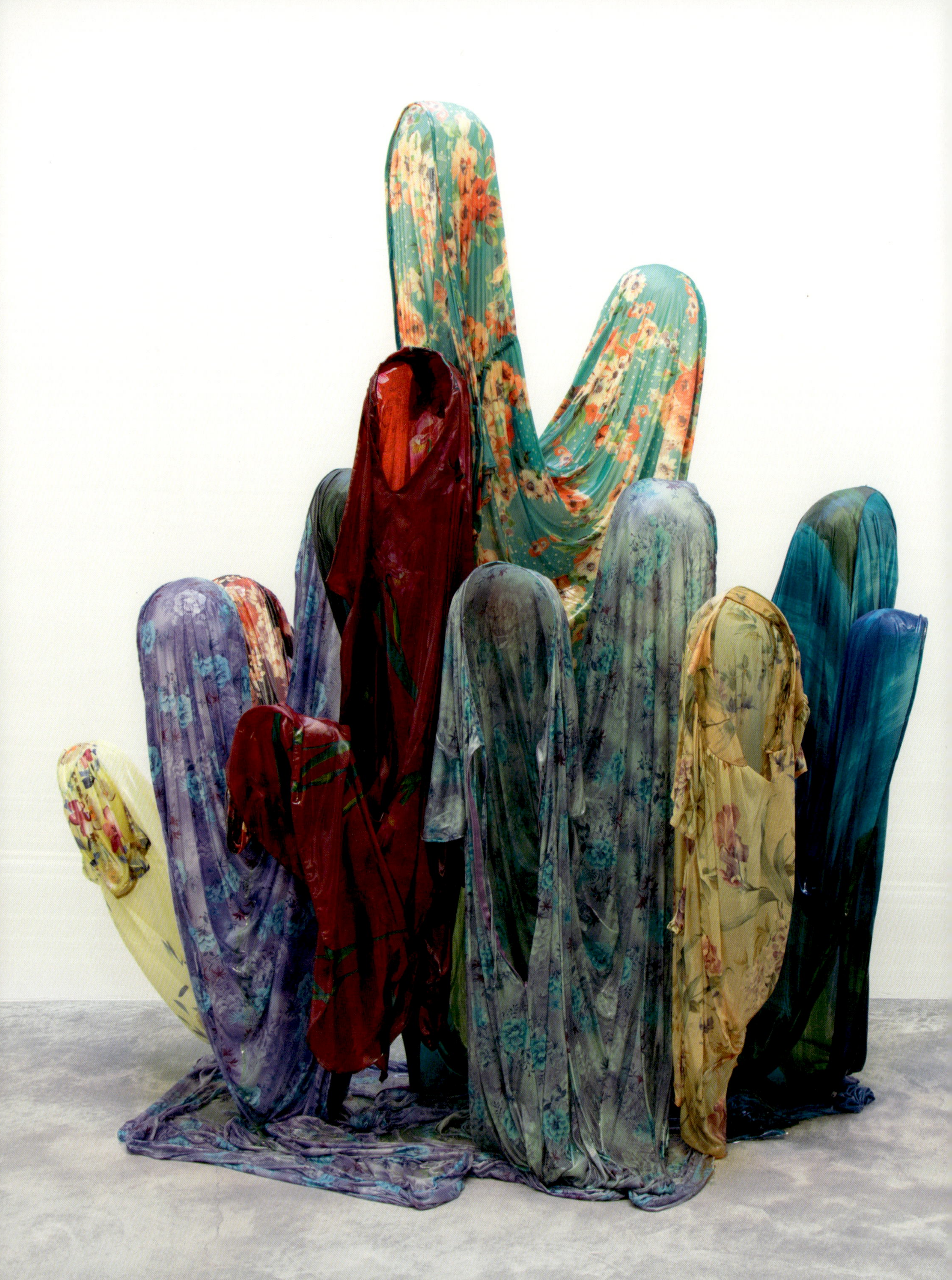

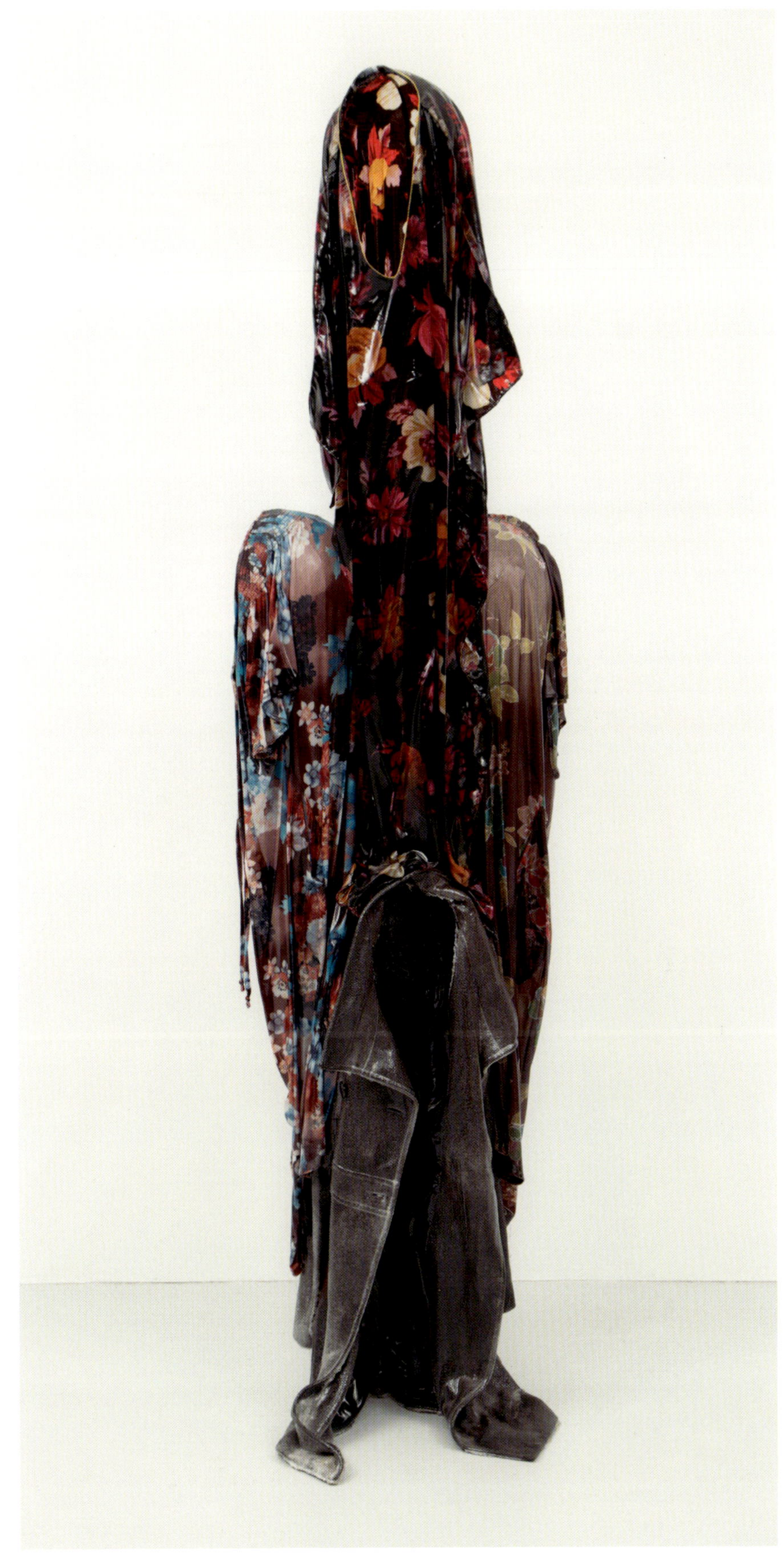

Opposite: *Untitled (hollow)*, 2016.
Resin, housedresses, and kaftans.
80 x 73 x 36 inches (203.2 x
185.4 x 91.4 cm). Albright-Knox
Art Gallery, Buffalo, NY. Albert H.
Tracy Fund, by exchange, 2016.

Untitled (Rhythm and Blues),
2016. Resin, housedresses,
kaftan, and a women's wool coat.
81 x 23 x 14 inches (205.7 x 58.4 x
35.6 cm). Collection of Hudgins
Family, New York.

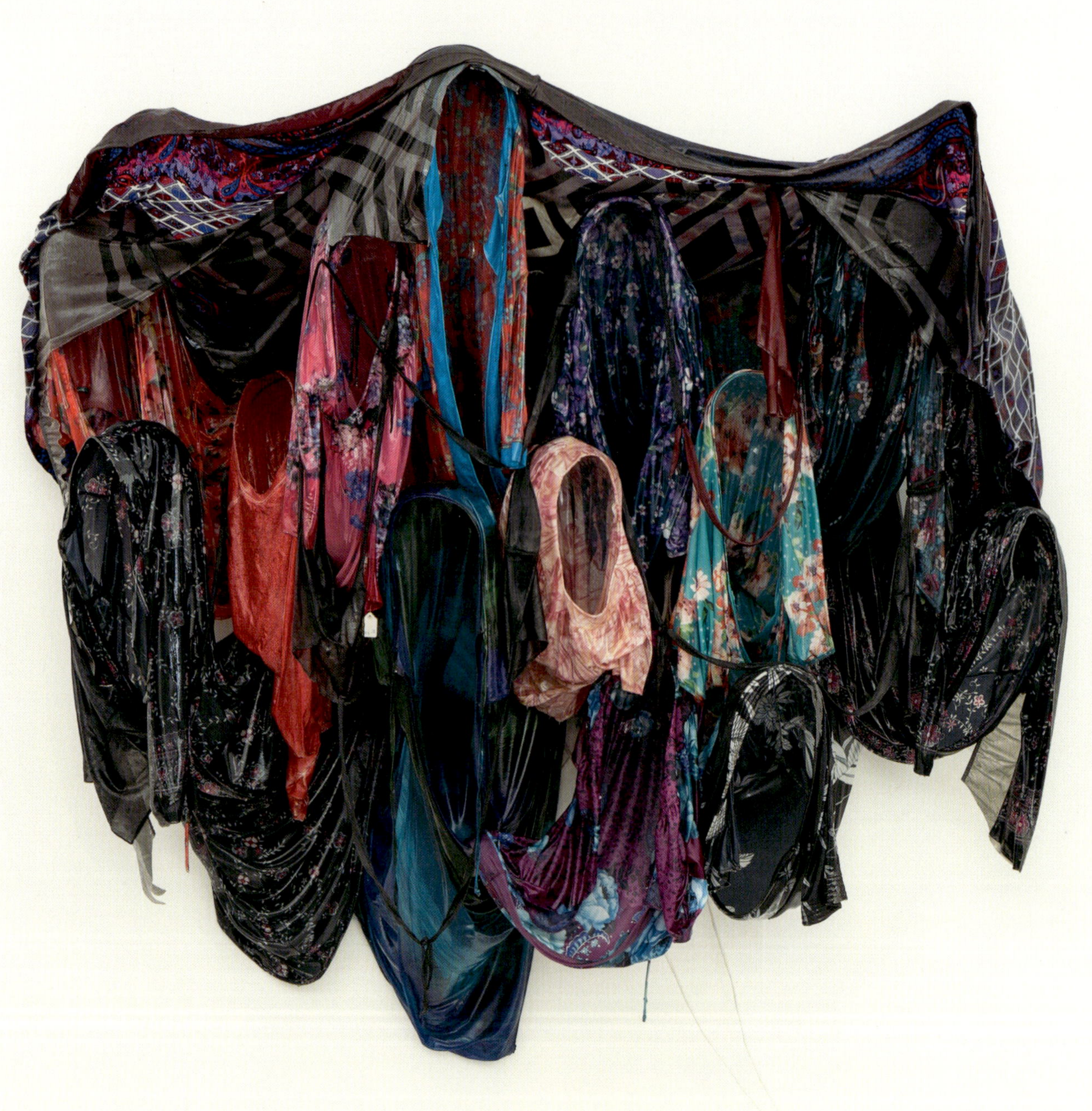

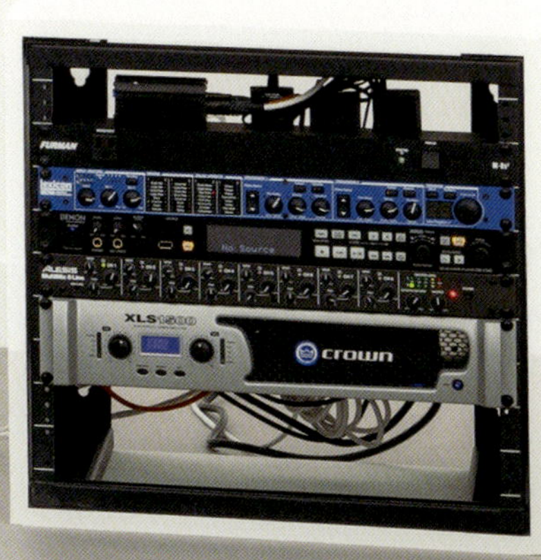

Phasing (Ebb), 2017.
Resin, housedresses, kaftans,
speakers, and audio equipment.
Dimensions variable. The Institute
of Contemporary Art/Boston.
Gift of Bridgitt and Bruce Evans.
Photo by Dawn Blackman.

The singular figure of *Untitled (. . . just watch)* begins to multiply into tight clusters of "ghosts," or groupings, that are suspended from the wall or stand on the floor. Their graceful swooping forms recall the robes of mourners or a choir, almost classical in appearance. In *Untitled (Sea)* (2016), eleven bodies reach out from the wall like shrouded heads emerging from a mass of blue housedresses. Each rounded volume is oriented slightly differently, and the strings of the dresses appear frozen mid-sway, endowing the sculpture with an incredible sense of movement and gesture. Many of Beasley's titles include references to music, such as *Untitled (Back-ups)* or *Untitled (Rhythm and Blues)* (both 2016). The cast shapes often possess uncanny connections to these short parenthetical elaborations: the harmony of the four bodies in *Back-ups*, or the inclusion of a wool coat as the base of *Rhythm and Blues*. Recently, Beasley experimented with combining sound equipment with his "ghost" sculptures, producing *Phasing (Ebb)* and *Phasing (Flow)* (both 2017). In these works, microphones placed at a distance from the colorful sculptures pick up the conversations and din of the environment. These sounds are processed by equipment sitting on the floor near the sculptures and then emitted from speakers hidden within the housedresses, T-shirts, and du-rags. A sheet covers each cluster as if the figures are huddled together, sheltering from rain. The distorted sounds ebb and flow, as the titles suggest, connecting viewers located in different places. The empty space is fundamental to the powerful effect of Beasley's "ghost" sculptures. As the voids stare out at us, we stare back. We see empty cavities and sense bodies once present. Light passes through the sculptures, making them appear to glow, and the colors turn brilliant.

Beasley's enmeshment in the optics and politics of air and breathing is also present in his performance work. For the installation and performance *Your face is / is not enough* (2016), the artist constructed elaborate headdresses around gas masks and encased megaphones in bulbous shapes, reimagining these studio tools and militaristic objects of safety and control. Each of the twelve figures has a distinctive style, ranging from the carnivalesque to the gothic and high pop. Materials used include guinea fowl feathers, an umbrella, a metal colander, and baseball cap bills detached and positioned like Mickey Mouse ears. For the installation, Beasley used some of the studio techniques he had developed in making his ghost sculptures, presenting the masks on microphone stands. The artist scored the piece to guide its activation. It begins with individuals wearing the masks and holding the megaphones; they lift the megaphone microphones up to the gas mask vents

Untitled (Sea), 2016. Resin and housedresses. 82 x 96 x 26.5 inches (208.3 x 243.8 x 67.3 cm). The Museum of Modern Art, New York. Gift of Marie-Josée and Henry R. Kravis.

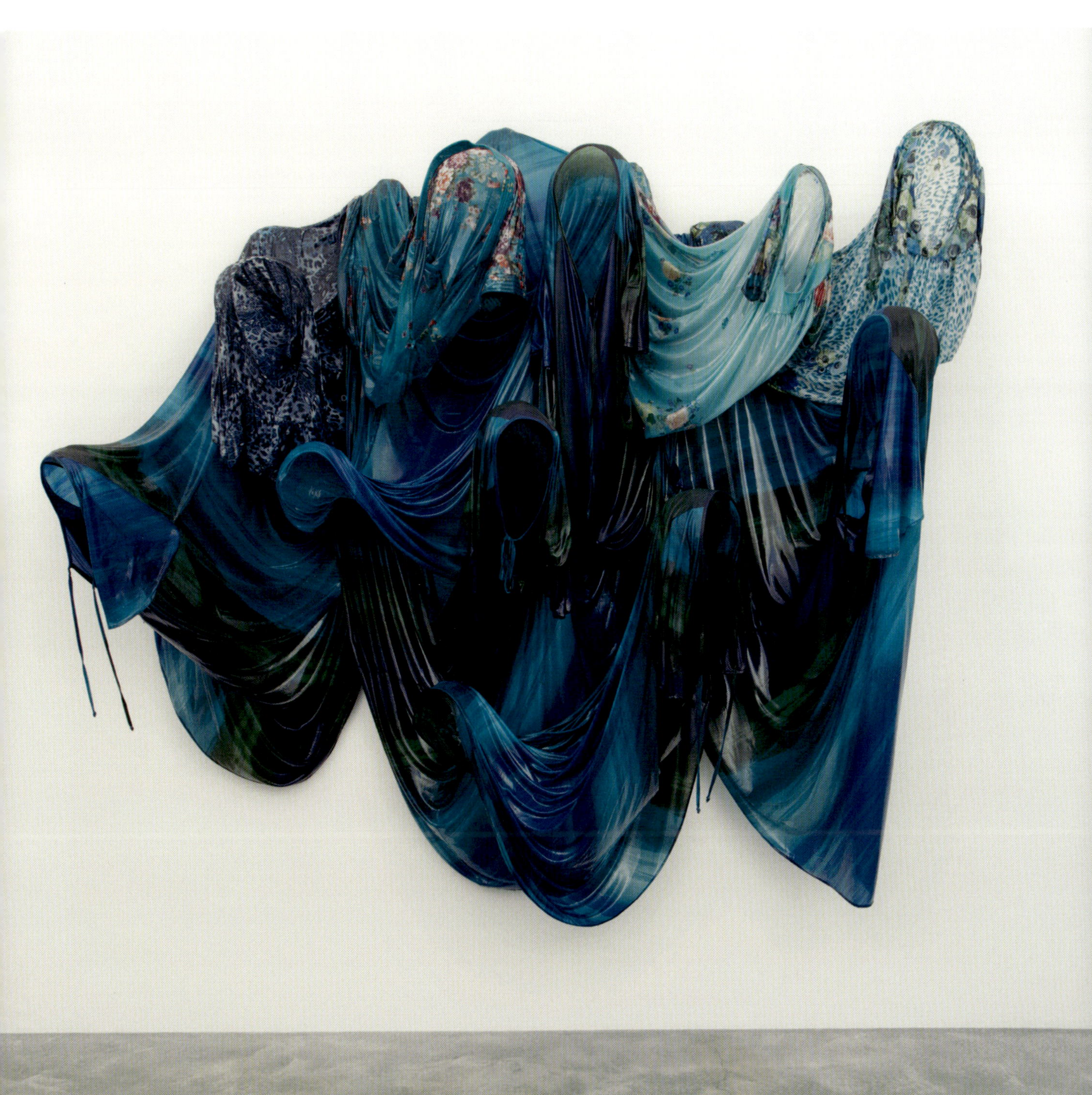

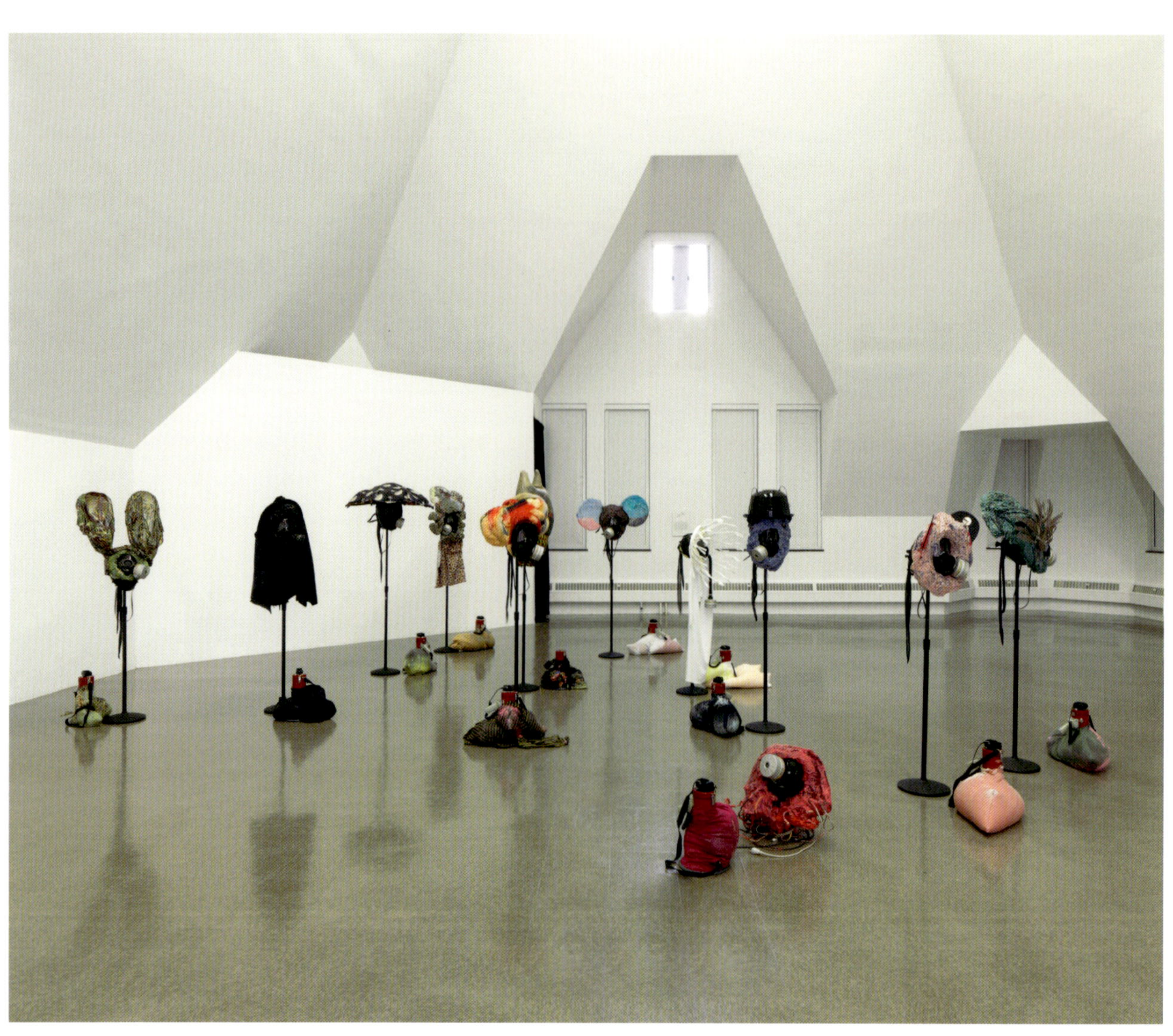

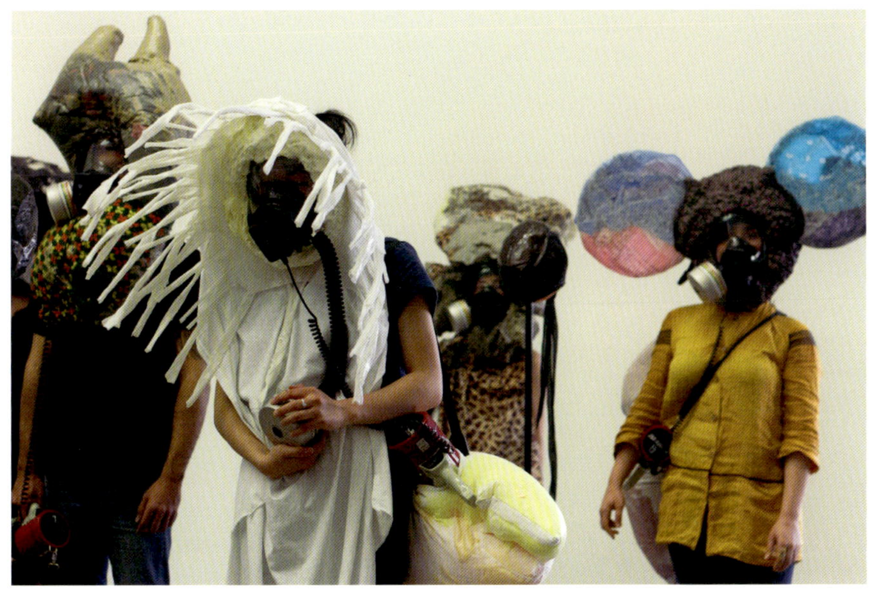

Performance view, *Your face is / is not enough*, 2016, The Renaissance Society at the University of Chicago, 2016. Image courtesy the *Hyde Park Herald*, Chicago. Photo by Spencer Bibbs.

and begin to breathe. Distorted through the mask and megaphone, the in-and-out of air sounds mechanical, wheezy, and thick. The performers begin with their own breathing rhythm and slowly sync up. Chests come to rise and fall together. The control and emphasis of the breath in this performance calls to mind a range of musical connotations, from the circular breathing of jazz horn players to the syncopated vocalized breathing in rap and beatboxing. Set against Eric Garner's dying words and the recurrence of Beasley's exploration of air, breath control might be a profound signifier of black cultural invention and simultaneously a symbol of the tragic deaths of so many black men and women.

Another recent work by Beasley, *Air Conditioner (Tempo)* (2017), overlays the droning blow of a window air conditioner unit with intermittent clips of political rallies, documentaries, and news coverage. The sculpture—a gutted window air-conditioner embedded in the middle of a wall—has two sides. Just as the ubiquitous window units circulate air between outside and inside, the sculpture connects two distinct places within the architectural environment (two separate rooms when it was installed in *Sport/Utility* at Casey Kaplan gallery). Beasley hones in on the object's essential function, not to mention its evident class and economic symbolism, as a starting point to remake ambient sound. The hum is no longer "white noise," vacant of meaning, but carries with it people's cries and stories, as captured and broadcast on radio and television. What is so striking about *Air Conditioner (Tempo)*, like all of Beasley's

Opposite: *Your face is / is not enough*, 2016. The Tate Americas Foundation, courtesy of the North American Acquisitions Committee in honour of Bob Rennie, Chair of the Committee 2010–2016, 2017. On long term loan. Installation view, *Between the Ticks of the Watch*, The Renaissance Society, University of Chicago, 2016. Image courtesy The Renaissance Society at the University of Chicago. Photo by Tom Van Eynde.

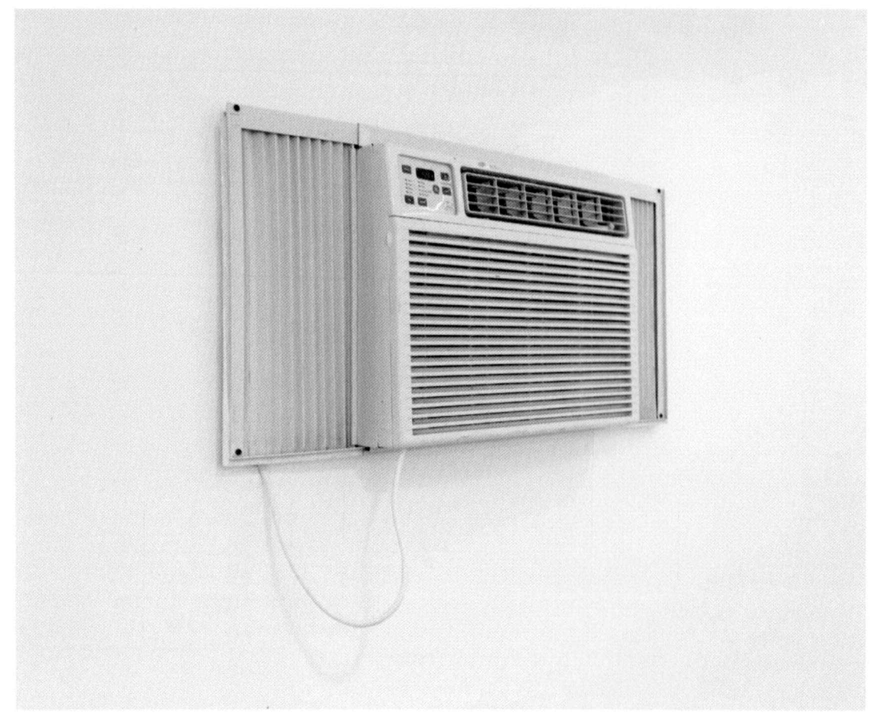

Air Conditioner (Tempo),
2017. Two-channel audio, air-
conditioner shell, custom
speakers, and audio equipment.
Dimensions variable. Rennie
Collection, Vancouver, BC.

work, is the artist's integration of culturally significant content and laden signifiers with his sensitive rendering of material. It connects spaces, literally within the gallery and metaphorically by bridging the public and the domestic, the collective and the personal: air, breath, and wind.

Beasley's most recent works, just finished at the time of my writing, are his "slab" works, which exist somewhere between sculpture and painting and are like containers for all of the ideas discussed thus far. For these artworks, the artist returns to laying clothing and objects into a mold and then pouring resin over them so that they stiffen and eventually stand. The process compresses clothing and other, odder things— so far, a hair roller, a mouth guard, and the side of a rolling shopping trolley—into a slab that is five or so inches thick. Patterns and colors appear like waves—coming and going—across the superflat surface of the works; the visible side is the one that would have been prone against the floor as Beasley laid down his materials. They read like impressions of an urban environment, as if Beasley somehow compressed the churning urban streets into an abstract landscape. One can imagine this studio work involves numerous choices and the element of chance. What objects shall be included? Are they personally significant? What will appear clearly once the soupy resin dries? What will be obscured?

Opposite: *Slab (Site/Picked A Constellation)*, 2017. House-dresses, kaftans, T-shirts, socks, du-rags, cotton, soil, bandanas, altered garments, altered fitted caps, and resin. 78¾ x 80 x 3 inches (200 x 203.2 x 7.6 cm). Hill Art Foundation, New York. Photo by Jason Wyche.

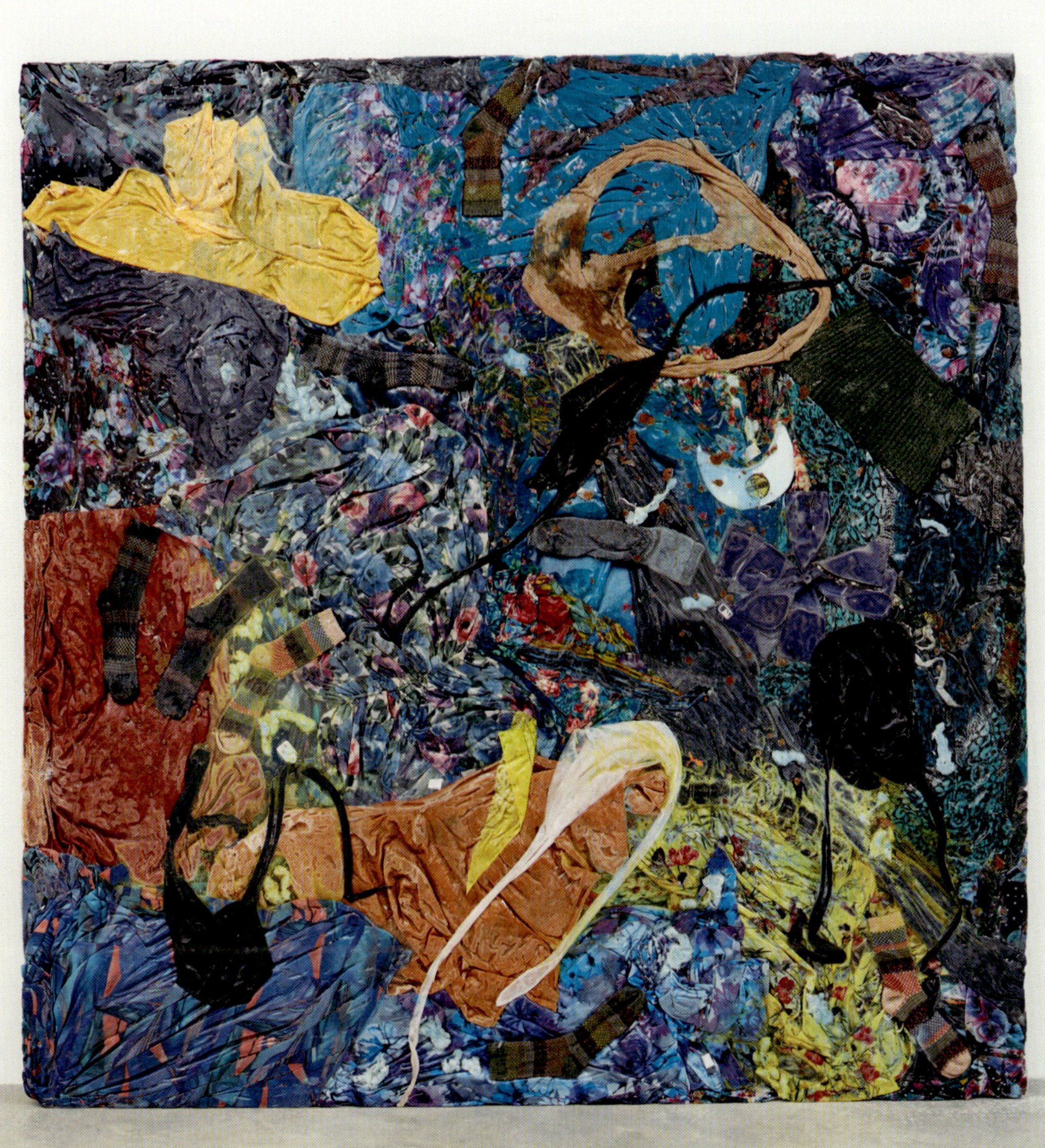

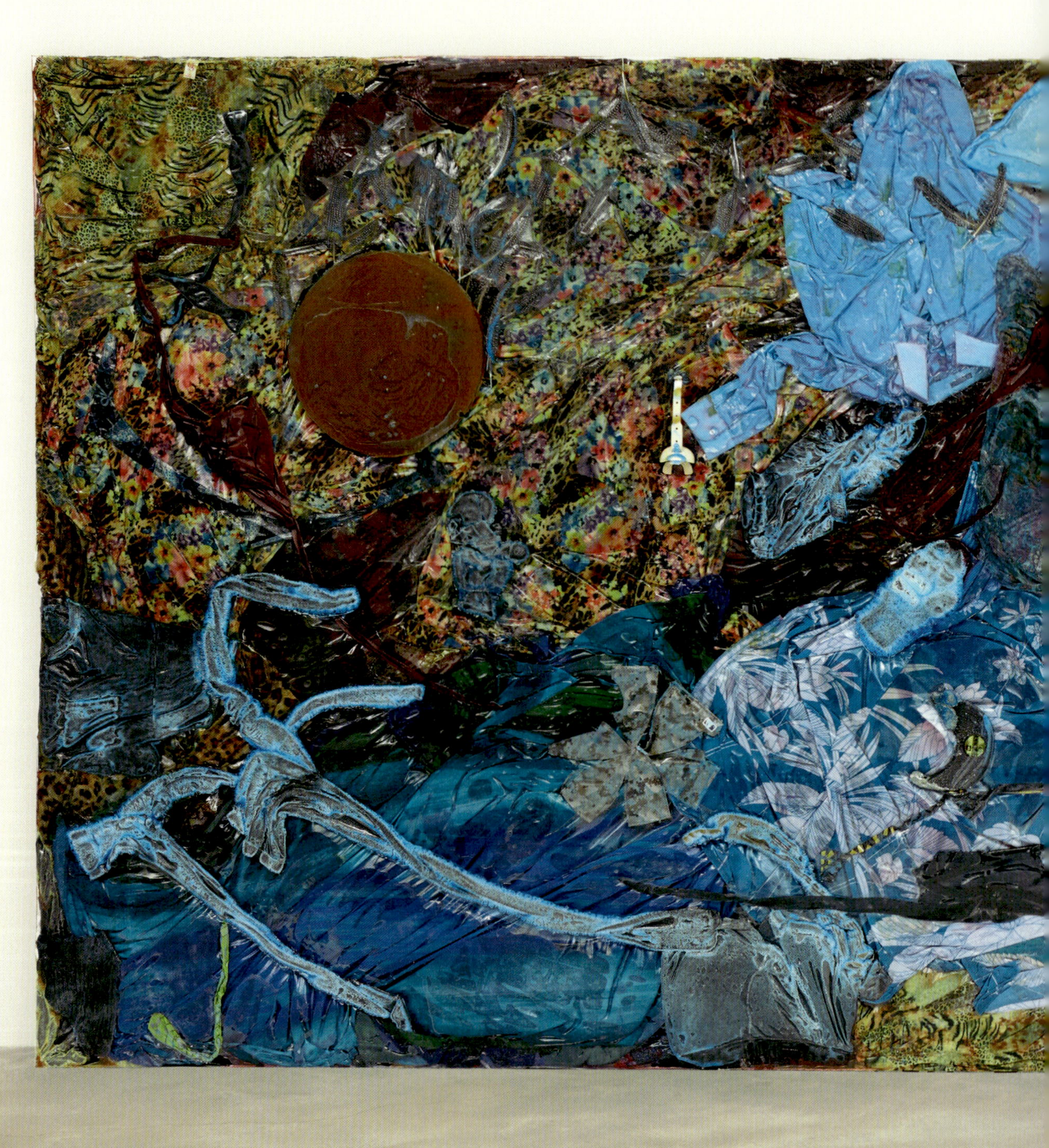

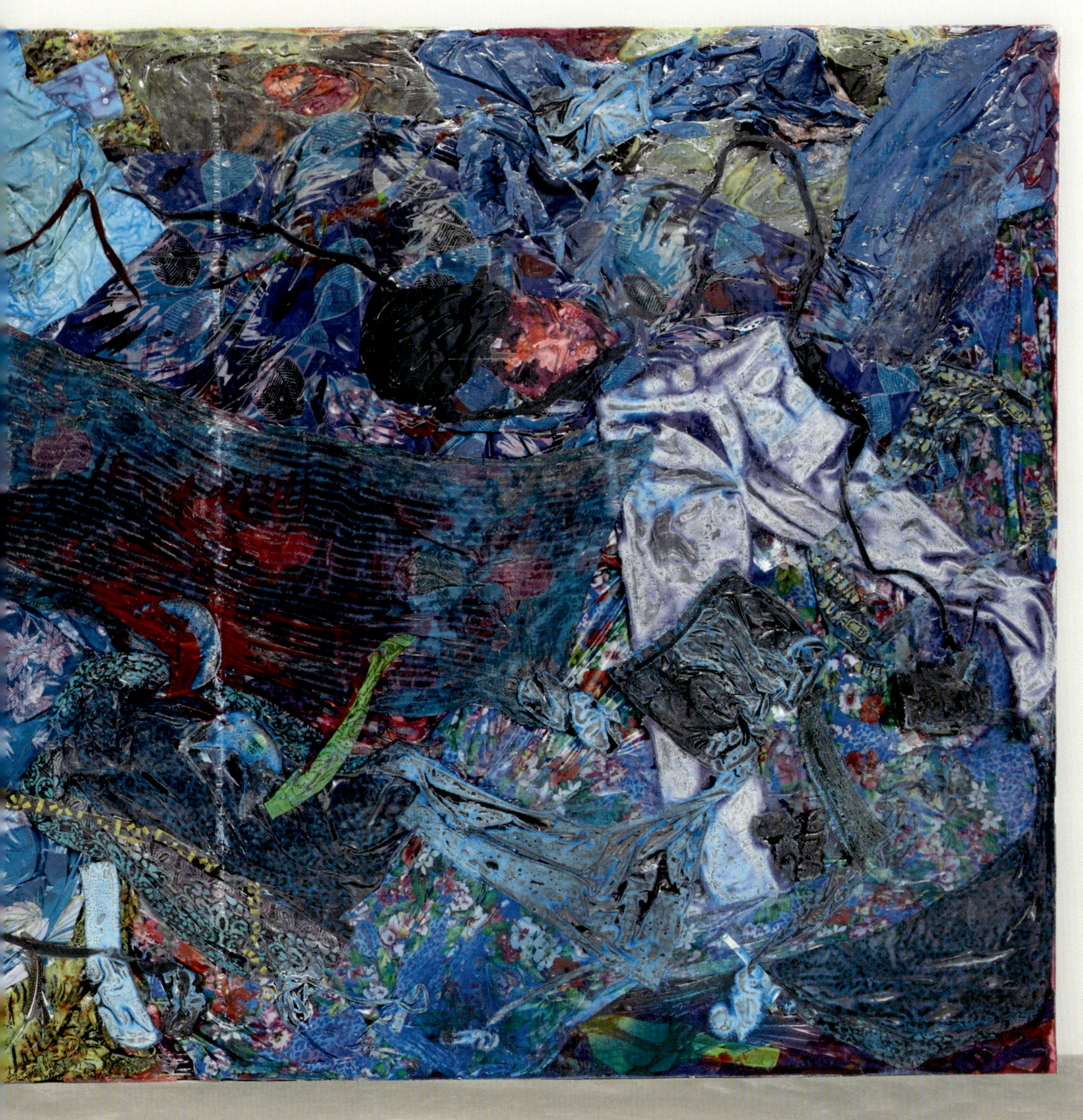

How will viewers relate to this slab and its contents? I imagine that Beasley does not know the answers to all of these questions, and I would wager that he is asking these and dozens of others. His practice allows for the space and time of the studio to matter and for the experience of the viewer to matter. It is through process that Beasley harnesses the communicative strength of symbols and then reconfigures those powerful forms to be open, vulnerable, and resilient. His work connects bodies in space—those present and those absent, whole and fractured, alone and entangled, black and white—to offer new forms and languages that express the human condition as we have inherited it and endeavor to reinvent it.

NOTES

1. Stuart Hall, "Encoding, Decoding," in *The Cultural Studies Reader*, ed. Simon During (New York: Routledge, 1993), 90–103.
2. Conversation with the artist, Queens, NY, March 22, 2017.
3. Conversation with Fred Abi-Hassoun, New York, September 13, 2017.
4. Ibid.
5. Jay-Z, "S. Carter," track 8 on *Vol. 3 . . . The Life and Times of S. Carter*, Roc-A-Fella/Def Jam, 1999.
6. At the invitation of the choreographer Ralph Lemon, Beasley's performance at the Museum of Modern Art, New York, took place on October 26, 2012.
7. At the invitation of the Museum of Contemporary Art, Cleveland, Beasley created four compositions for different parts of the day—sunrise, high noon, sundown, and nighttime—that were performed in the condemned Cozad-Bates House for a small audience. The site-specific performance, *And in My Dream I Was Rolling on the Floor*, took place on April 12, 2014, between 6:45 a.m. and 8:45 p.m.
8. At the invitation of Cleopatra's in Brooklyn, Beasley's exhibition, *. . . all different: for I do, I suppose, partake of multitude*, took place at the gallery Interstate Projects, Brooklyn, NY, June 14–30, 2013.
9. Press release for *. . . all different: for I do, I suppose, partake of multitude* at Interstate Projects, Brooklyn, NY, 2013, curated by Cleopatra's.
10. Conversation with the artist, Queens, NY, March 22, 2017.
11. "History of Lynchings," NAACP, accessed October 19, 2017, http://www.naacp.org/history-of-lynchings/.
12. Christina Sharpe, *In the Wake: On Blackness and Being* (Chapel Hill, NC: Duke University Press, 2016), 14.
13. See "12-Year-Old Boy Dies After Police in Cleveland Shoot Him," *New York Times*, November 23, 2014, https://www.nytimes.com/2014/11/24/us/boy-12-dies-after-being-shot-by-cleveland-police-officer.html?_r=0; "Tragedy Gives the Hoodie a Whole New Meaning," March 24, 2013, NPR, http://www.npr.org/2012/03/24/149245834/tragedy-gives-the-hoodie-a-whole-new-meaning; and Al Baker, J. David Goodman, and Benjamin Mueller, "Beyond the Chokehold: The Path to Eric Garner's Death," *New York Times*, June 13, 2015, https://www.nytimes.com/2015/06/14/nyregion/eric-garner-police-chokehold-staten-island.html.
14. A key precedent here is David Hammons's *In the Hood* (1993), a sculpture consisting of the detached hood of a green hoodie sweatshirt.

Previous: *A view of a reflection*, 2017. Housedresses, kaftans, T-shirts, socks, du-rags, bandanas, altered garments, altered fitted caps, altered bedsheet, mouthguards, feathers, and resin. 82¼ x 178 x 5¼ inches (208.9 x 452.1 x 13.3 cm). The Komal Shah and Gaurav Garg Collection, Atherton, CA. Photo by Jason Wyche.

Movement V: Ballroom, 2017. Performance at the Eldorado Ballroom, Houston, Project Row Houses and Cynthia Woods Mitchell Center for the Arts, University of Houston, 2017. Courtesy Cynthia Woods Mitchell Center for the Arts, University of Houston. Photo by dabphoto creative.

Overleaf: *Chair of the Ministers of Defense*, 2016, and *Untitled (Curtain)*, 2016. Installation view, *Hammer Projects: Kevin Beasley*, Hammer Museum, Los Angeles, 2017. Rennie Collection, Vancouver, BC. Photo by Brian Forrest.

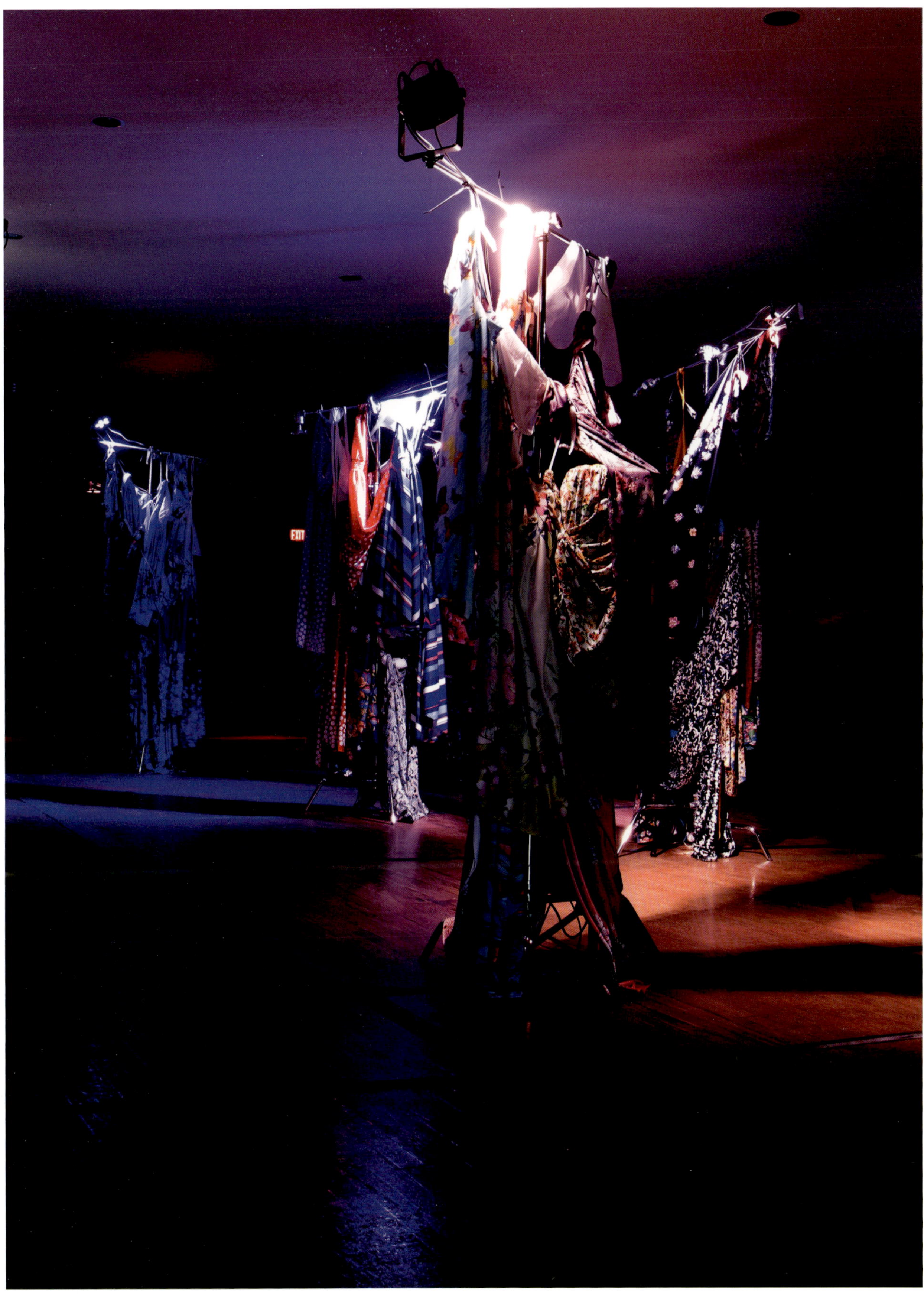

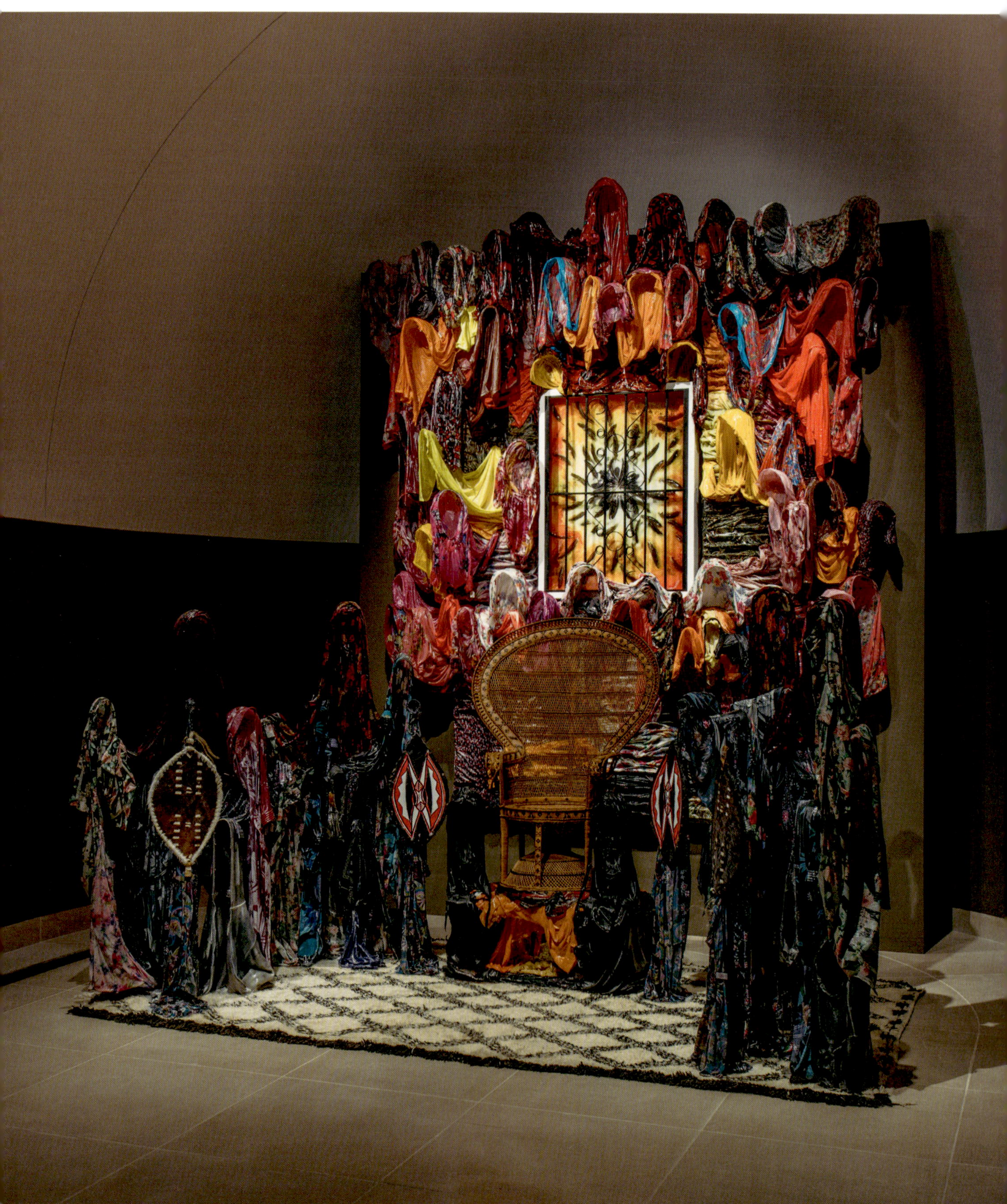

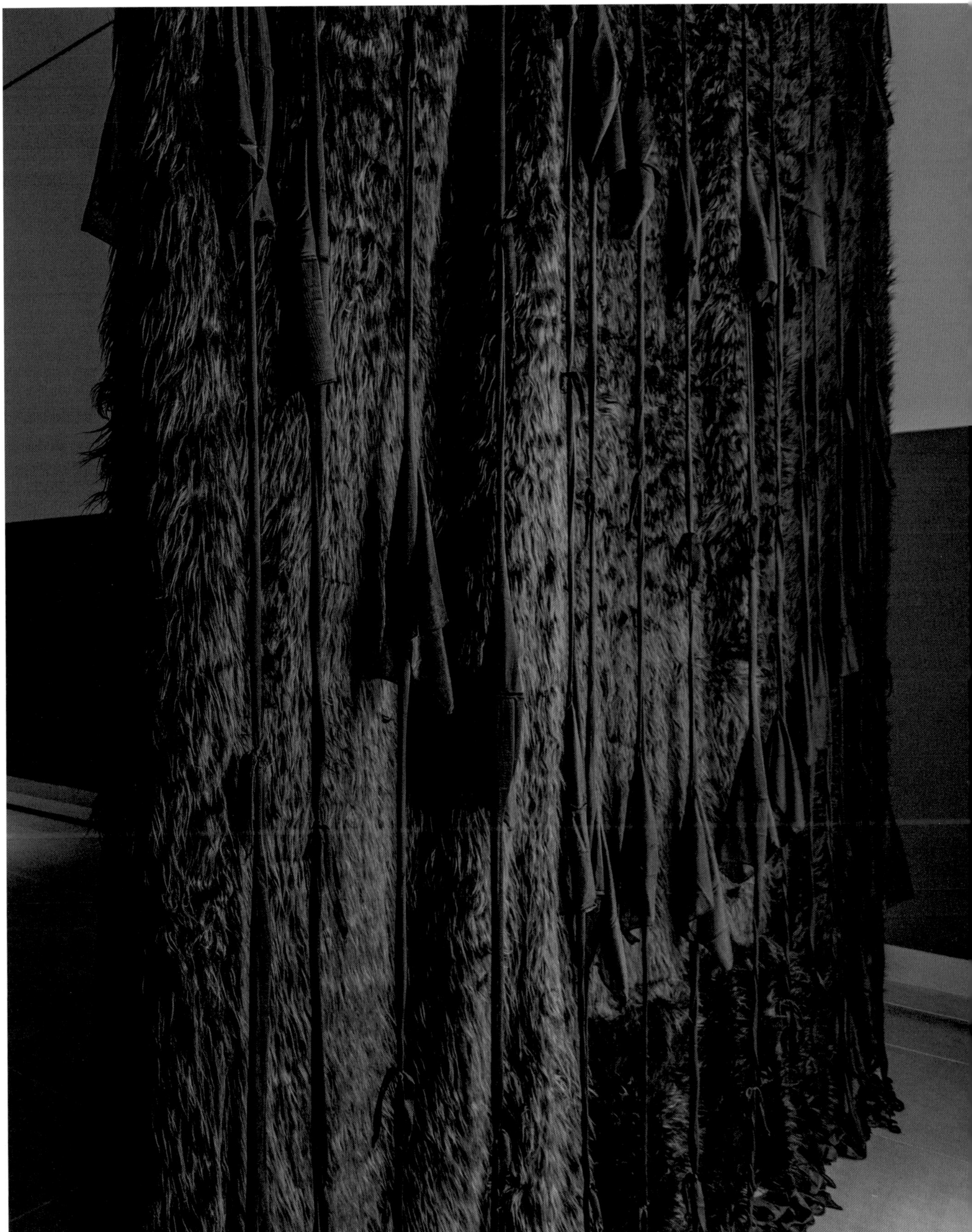

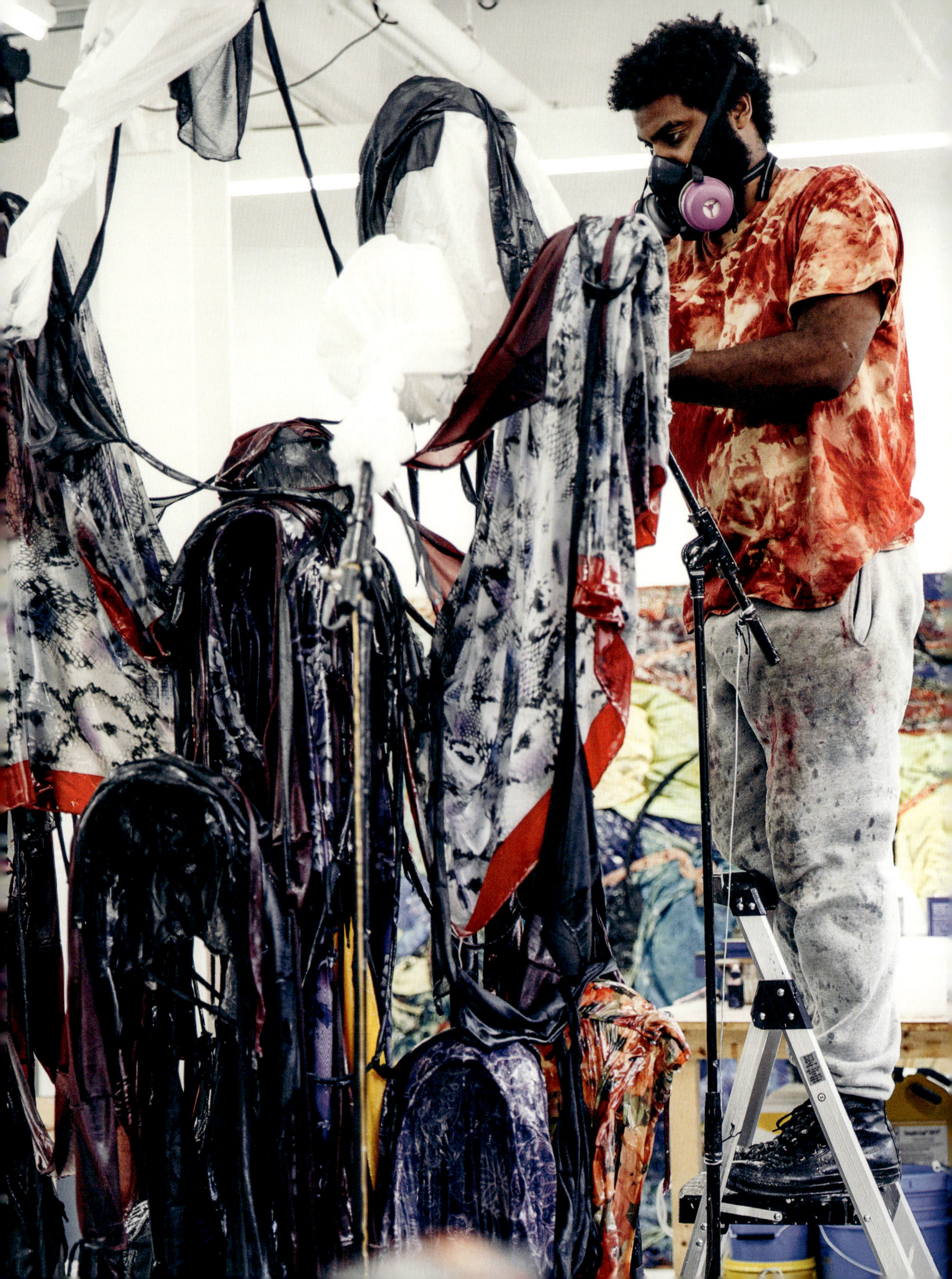

In Conversation
Kevin Beasley and Mark Bradford

Kevin Beasley   We first met in the spring of 2012 when I was doing my MFA at Yale, and you were a visiting artist there. It was so generative, and there was an immediate connection, so as a starting point for our conversation I wanted to return to some of the concerns you raised, and the subject of the studio. When you came into my studio, I remember that I almost immediately started getting into the social and political content of my work, and you interjected by recognizing my investment in these relationships but insisted that I look at an even broader picture within my practice and, more specifically, not box the work in. I'm paraphrasing here, but you said that people always try to categorize you and see you in a way they want to, particularly as a black artist, so it's important to allow the aspects of your interests that are outside of stereotypes of the black identity to surface—that which is unexpected. A lot has occurred since 2012, so as an attempt to check in on these ideas, I'm curious about how this continues to factor into *your* decisions in the studio, if at all?

Mark Bradford   Did I, at Yale? Well, good. What struck me when I first entered your studio was your thought process, and your investigation of materials. Yes, black artists really have to "claim" that space of fluidity as we work through our ideas and investigate, to be able to say: "I'm figuring my shit out." I would look at the sculptures and your fascination with music as a jumping-off point for a kind of meditation. And I remember

Kevin Beasley in his studio, Queens, NY, 2017. Photo by Patrick Daly.

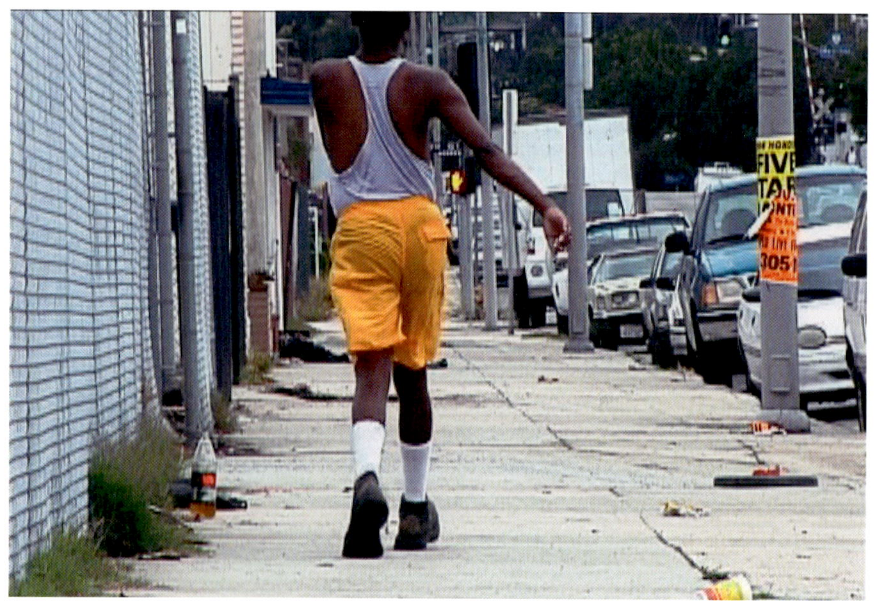

you being very clear about what your interests were and I think since then you have stood firm. That's why your work rings true. Oftentimes what we learn in grad school is a theoretical European gaze, as if nothing or anything else would or should be the impetus for the work. But I believe that being black demands a kind of doublespeak/double consciousness à la [W. E. B.] Du Bois. The black male body is one of the most politicized bodies in the USA. How can we turn fully away from the political, social, and national debates?

KB   I would even suggest that the attempt to turn away, if that was an interest, would have to recognize the social and political debates in order to know from what one is turning. It's just not a useful exercise to turn one's back on these issues without a sense of their trajectory. This is one reason why your video work *Niagara* (2015) in the American Pavilion at the 2017 Venice Biennale was so resonant, because it embedded this double consciousness—within the work there is a walking-away from the gaze and yet toward something beyond our sight and vision: the man's gait actually suggested a sense of resolve, something more generative and internally resolute. It's a very nuanced and multilayered work in that context, because it produced an image of representation that laid claim to this fluidity. You made visible the act of walking away from the gaze. I saw its function as parallel to the treatment of the building itself,

Mark Bradford, *Niagara* (still), 2006. Video (color, sound; 3:17 minutes). Courtesy the artist and Hauser & Wirth, Los Angeles, © Mark Bradford.

within which abstracted gestures could take on multiple reads with a kind of sociopolitical awareness. For example, can one see within the work a level of awareness to these concerns within abstract gestures and forms without prior knowledge of that interest/relationship? What is being abstracted? And how does that action continue to carry the cultural weight of those materials? I think this is why I have an interest in this kind of abstraction, the kind that utilizes these cultural materials as a mode of exploration. I ask these questions when working with music and sound clips—does the audio from a significant/tragic political event still carry its importance when it is recontextualized? How much abstraction can this go through before it loses its immediacy? Or even urgency? Because I really think that an audio recording of a riot has a particular rhythm and timbre.

MB   Can you talk a little more about your use of materials? It seems that you have such a rich array, a mature gaze. How did that develop?

KB   Materials are always an expanding aspect of my practice, because as much as I enjoy the technical understanding of how these things come together, I am constantly questioning what can be a viable material to use, to explore the ideas I am engaging with. Materials sometimes drive an artwork and at other times they are the by-product of an experience I've had that either left me vulnerable, or left me unable to express something about that experience with words. For example, seeing a cotton field for the very first time in my life left me speechless, not just because of slavery and the American cotton field, but also because of its materiality—its transformation, yet its essential quality. A cotton blanket isn't that far removed from a raw cotton boll—there is actually very little noticeable processing. That direct transformation is very important because at its core, it is unlike anything else. There are no substitutes when you consider the entire life of the material. So I am constantly thinking about how I get to an understanding of my surround-ings (people, places, and such) in all of their nuances. It is how I end up using housedresses and kaftans in some work and then a crushed Cadillac Escalade in another—they are both connected to my navigation of the world because I've had compelling questions about those objects, people who have had an impact in my life, and the effects of society on the way I am perceived/perceive myself. It's myriad; I become over-whelmed by the varying levels of emphasis placed on subjects, context,

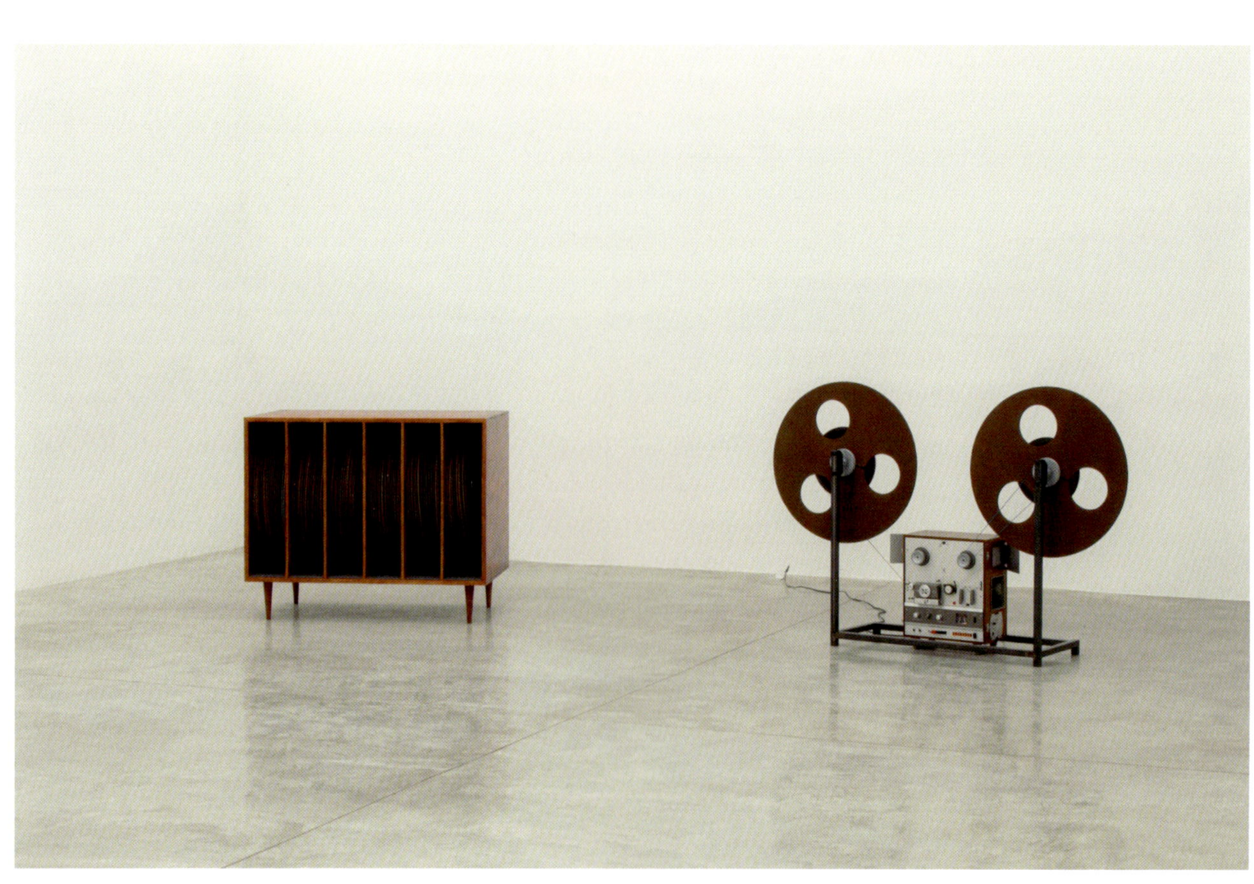

and how much that can fluctuate in the process, but I'm constantly trying to develop and refine my approach. Something that worked for me in the studio a year or two ago just may not now, because my thinking and knowledge about certain materials evolves.

MB   Your projects generally have such a strong materiality; how do you connect these with your work with sound, music, vinyl? Are these an expansion of your practice, or did this work develop simultaneously?

KB   I've played drums since I was thirteen, and I have some basic sheet-music-reading ability, but for the longest time, I'd always kept my music separate from art. The lines began to blur while I was in graduate school, specifically because of my increasing interest in vinyl and mixing. Mixing was really the "aha" moment, because I'd never thought about how tactile, how physical, and how transformable sound and music could be through vinyl. Once I'd invested a bit of my student loan money into some DJ equipment, it all became another set of sculptural tools. I saw them in the same way I viewed any of my other tools and materials, except instead of plaster, resin, or clothing, it was recordings and the sound waves of various frequencies. What I had worked so hard to keep separate for the sake of some kind of purity became the very thing I needed to break down and mix up. So in one way, my practice is invested in the discovery of these connective aspects of materiality.

I've become especially interested in recorded sound because it provides us with a mark of time, like an etching in a wall or an ancient relief. It becomes materially significant because it describes the condition of a space through other means than our sense of seeing, which we rely on so heavily to navigate the world. I just can't continue to move through society without asking questions about what I'm hearing, what is being said, the noise of the world. I could go on forever about it, but I will say this: the immediate urgency I find in sound—even more so when it comes from a physical object such as vinyl—is the necessity to listen and give it time and space. It's so much about observation and actually submitting to what is being projected, and that is a very vulnerable and revealing space to commit to, because you open yourself up to hearing something you may not understand, like, or agree with. If there was more of an emphasis focused listening, I think we could begin to understand more nuance in our daily encounters, effectively refining our relationships with one another and with the world we inhabit.

MB So with mixing and vinyl becoming sculptural tools, how did you begin to craft a language around them? I mean, there ain't a lot of people using this particular toolbox. I remember DJ Spooky [Paul Miller] years ago—nothing like what you do, but his name comes to mind. There is always a sense of purity, isn't there? Blur, remix, and acceleration always come to my mind when I'm looking at your work. I remember the earlier sculptures, and then the shift to mixing, and I noticed there was a lot of buzz and I thought: I hope he keeps going. I love that you did and that you keep pushing.

KB Language can be tough for me because I always feel like what I'm describing is still not what is happening, or that the words I am finding are foundational to something else that is more interesting and/or relevant. Working with vinyl, I was literally looking for words to describe the techniques—kind of a pun right there, since the Technics SL-1200 is the industry standard turntable for DJs—for mixing and so much of DJing, and mixing language relates to art making. Scratching has two important meanings to me in both music and in making sculptures, not to mention the word *mixing*. I do think a practice of questioning is essential, and a lot of questions were produced, but I want some answers along the way, too. I think the words I cling to are those answers I've found within a much bigger trajectory. I've also wanted to ask you about this because you find language so naturally. It's really sharp, funny, but also really relatable—even when speaking about adversity, your approach is very uplifting. How do you think about language in relationship to your artworks and your practice?

MB I agree—language is always a bit late to the party, isn't it? I think you do a good job of leaving room for a certain fluidity, much like your mixing. What is always the challenge is to maintain that sense of fluidity as you change and grow. Language is not and will not ever be perfect. It's like that childhood friend you should have dropped long ago but you still cling to the childhood memories although you've been let down a million times. That's language for me: flawed. But I often use humor to skate along the edge of an idea, to maybe push it into a space that is a little more uncomfortable under the guise of "ha ha ha." Really, you find out what fits after you kill the theoretical "daddy" that sits on all of our shoulders post–grad school. I'm curious to know where you are now. You've been out of school for a few years now and are critically questioning things.

*If I was standing alone
I wouldn't stand it at all*, 2017.
Housedresses, kaftans,
T-shirts, du-rags, and resin.
99¾ x 53 x 53 inches
(253.4 x 134.6 x 134.6 cm).
San Antonio Museum of Art,
purchased with The Brown
Foundation Contemporary Art
Acquisition Fund. Photo by
Jason Wyche.

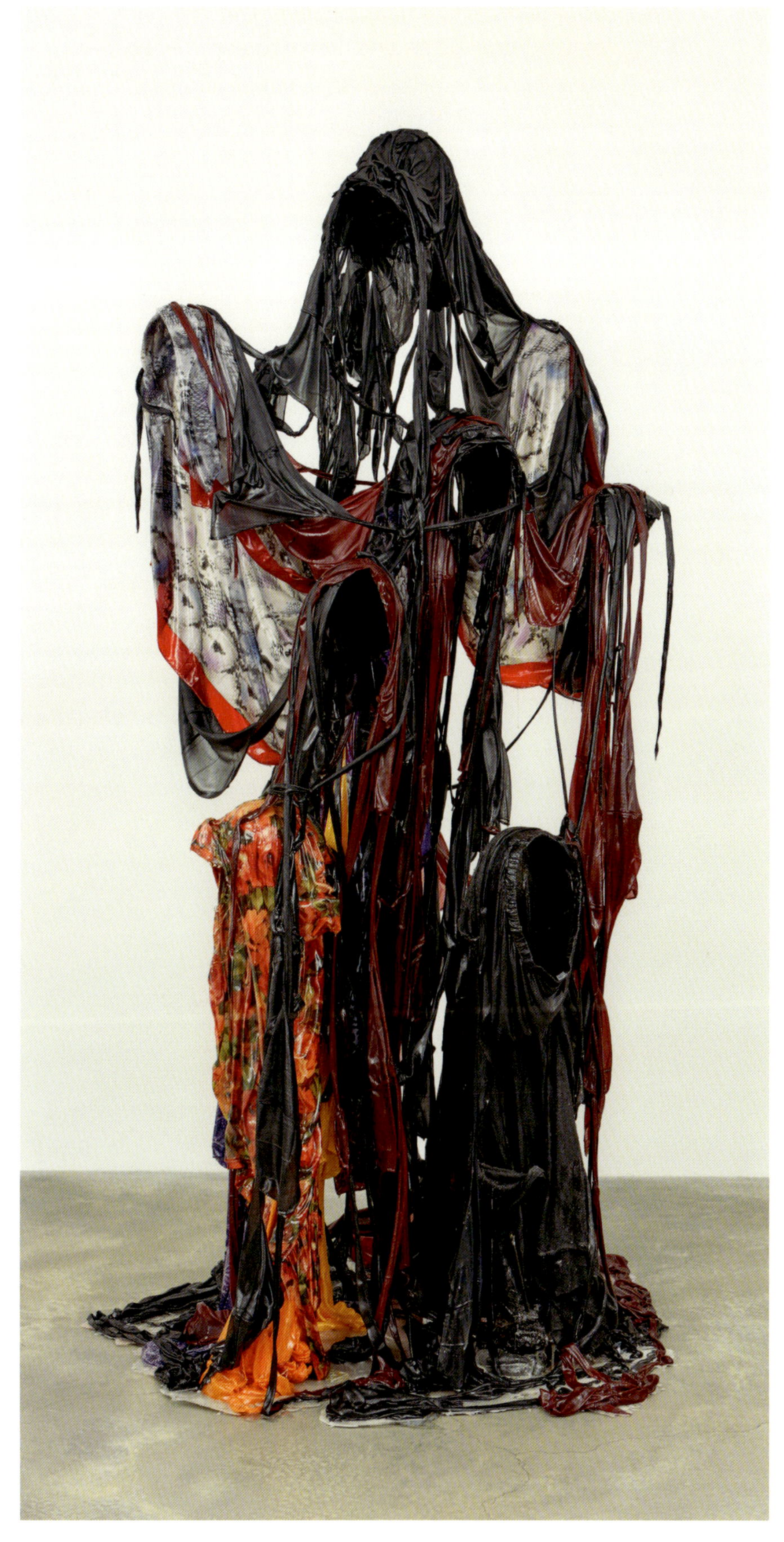

Does it affect how you think about how to use language, or what has
recently changed?

KB   I definitely feel the weight of the theory daddy, even though I never read
much theory—I'm not good at recalling references and names, and it
is taking me time to let my emotions and senses take over rather than
my mind and analysis. It's an ongoing battle and shows up in the way I
try to speak about it. But I do feel a change, and in fact, while I was in
grad school I had these heavy emotional experiences. It made me think,
Okay—this is the potent stuff that I can't rationalize, nor can I ignore it,
and most importantly, I really didn't understand it. In the years since grad
school, it has been so much about how to be someone who is critically
questioning things via these emotions and feelings. And really, I would
say that the critical questioning I'm engaged in is a severe case of skep-
ticism about where I am in society. There is true value in those feelings,
especially if you're an affectionate and passionate person, which I
consider myself to be. I just hope to develop a collection of words and
experiences that can be read by others who can relate and connect with
them, and maybe that can breed a generative society.

Sport/Utility, 2017.
Stripped and crushed
Cadillac Escalade ESV.
65½ x 93 x 203 inches
(166.4 x 236.2 x 515.6 cm).

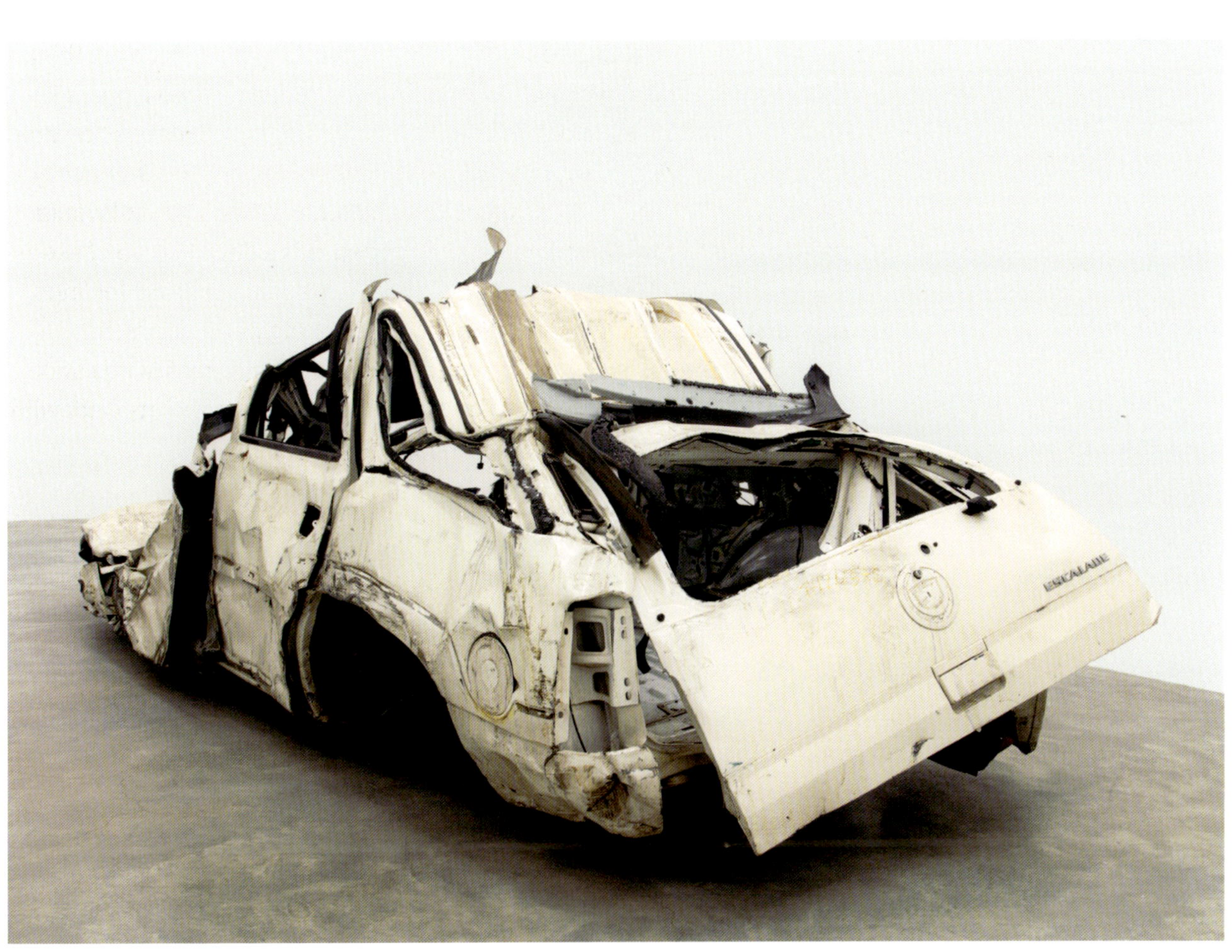

Biography

Born in Lynchburg, VA, 1985
Lives and works in New York

Education

2012
MFA, Yale University School of Art,
New Haven, CT

2007
BFA, College for Creative Studies, Detroit

Solo Exhibitions

2018
Whitney Museum of American Art, New York

2017
Rubbings, kim? Contemporary Art Centre,
Riga, Latvia
Sport/Utility, Casey Kaplan, New York
Movement V: Ballroom, CounterCurrent17, in
collaboration with Project Row Houses and
the Cynthia Woods Mitchell Center for the
Arts, University of Houston
Hammer Projects: Kevin Beasley, Hammer
Museum, Los Angeles

2016
inHarlem: Kevin Beasley, The Studio Museum in
Harlem, New York

2015
Untitled Stanzas: Staff/Un/Site, High Line at the
Rail Yards, New York

Night (1947–2015), curated by Jordan Stein,
The Glass House, New Canaan, CT
Kevin Beasley, Casey Kaplan, New York

2014
Kevin Beasley, The Butcher's Daughter, Detroit

2012
Latency: A Collection of Works by Kevin Beasley,
The Butcher's Daughter, Ferndale, MI

2009
Found Asleep Underwater, ORG Contemporary,
Detroit

2008
Non/Places, Neal Davis Gallery, Royal Oak, MI

Performances

2017
Movement V: Ballroom, CounterCurrent17, in
collaboration with Project Row Houses and
the Cynthia Woods Mitchell Center for the
Arts, University of Houston

2016
*Visual Artists at the Atrium: Michel Auder and
Kevin Beasley*, David Rubenstein Atrium,
Lincoln Center for the Performing Arts,
New York
*Movement II: BEATEN-FACE/TOMS/ARMS,
TIES, & LEG/FLOOR/BODY/BASS*,
Art Gallery of Ontario, Toronto

Your face is / is not enough, The Renaissance
Society at the University of Chicago

2015
Scaffold Room, The Kitchen, New York
Untitled Stanzas: Staff/Un/Site, High Line at the
Rail Yards, New York
An Evening with Kevin Beasley, Solomon R.
Guggenheim Museum, New York
Black Rocker, Dallas Museum of Art, presented
by SOLUNA International Arts Festival and
Dallas Museum of Art
Movement IV, Casey Kaplan, New York

2014
*Movement II: BEATEN-FACE/TOMS/ARMS,
TIES, & LEG/FLOOR/BODY/BASS*,
New Forms Festival, Vancouver, BC
*Movement I: DEF/ACHE/CRYSTALLINE/
SLEEVE*, Whitney Biennial, Whitney Museum
of American Art, New York
Casey Kaplan, New York
And in My Dream I Was Rolling on the Floor,
Museum of Contemporary Art, Cleveland
Walker Art Center, Minneapolis. Presented in
conjunction with *Sound Horizon,* curated by
Jim Hodges
From Ashy to Classy Mix I (Valley of Ashes),
Queens Museum of Art, NY

2013
*. . . all different: for I do, I suppose, partake of
multitude*, organized by Cleopatra's, Interstate
Projects, Brooklyn, NY

2012
I Want My Spot Back, Museum of Modern Art,
New York

Group Exhibitions

2018
Beautiful World, where are you?, Liverpool
Biennial, Liverpool, UK
Inherent Structure, Wexner Center for the Arts,
The Ohio State University, Columbus, OH

2017
*Solidary & Solitary: The Joyner/Giuffrida
Collection*, US traveling exhibition
(through 2019)
*That I am reading backwards and into for a
purpose, to go on:*, curated by the Whitney
Museum of American Art Independent Study
Program, The Kitchen, New York

2016
A Slow Succession with Many Interruptions,
San Francisco Museum of Modern Art
The Beat Goes On, curated by Derrick Adams,
SVA Chelsea Gallery, New York
Blackness in Abstraction, curated by Adrienne
Edwards, Pace Gallery, New York
*Imitation of Life: Melodrama and Race in the
21st Century*, HOME, Manchester, UK
Between the Ticks of the Watch, curated by
Solveig Øvstebø, The Renaissance Society at
the University of Chicago
Surrogates, Griffin Art Projects, Vancouver, BC

KALEIDOSCOPE: A Moment of Grace,
    Modern Art Oxford, UK
A Shape That Stands Up, curated by Jamillah
    James, Hammer Museum at Art + Practice
    Foundation, Los Angeles
Winter 2015: Collected Works, Rennie Museum,
    Vancouver, BC
Looking Back / The 10th White Columns Annual,
    selected by Matthew Higgs, White Columns,
    New York

2015

*Many Things Brought from One Climate to
    Another*, Art Gallery of Ontario, Toronto
Greater New York, MoMA PS1, Queens, NY
*Breath/Breadth: Contemporary American
    Black Male Identity*, Maier Museum of Art at
    Randolph College, Lynchburg, VA
Storylines: Contemporary Art at the Guggenheim,
    Solomon R. Guggenheim Museum, New York

2014

Africa Now: Political Patterns, Seoul Museum of
    Art, South Korea
Cut to Swipe, Museum of Modern Art, New York
Rockaway!, MoMA PS1, Queens, NY
Material Histories, The Studio Museum in Harlem,
    New York
*When the Stars Begin to Fall: Imagination and
    the American South*, The Studio Museum in
    Harlem, New York; NSU Museum of Art, Fort
    Lauderdale, FL; the Institute of Contemporary
    Art/Boston

Whitney Biennial, Whitney Museum of American
    Art, New York
Harold Ancart, Kevin Beasley, Mateo López,
    Casey Kaplan, New York

2013

Queens International 2013, Queens Museum of
    Art, Queens, NY
Realization is Better than Anticipation, Museum of
    Contemporary Art, Cleveland
6<<<>>>6 Part I, Interstate Projects,
    Brooklyn, NY

2012

Fore, The Studio Museum in Harlem, New York
Some Sweet Day, Museum of Modern Art,
    New York
Thesis Part Two, Yale University Art Gallery,
    New Haven, CT
An All Day Event. The End, Danspace Project,
    New York

2011

New Departures and Transitions, N'Namdi Center
    for Contemporary Art, Detroit
*College Art Association New York Area MFA
    Exhibition*, Hunter College, New York

2010

Paycheck to Paycheck, The Butcher's Daughter,
    Ferndale, MI

2009

Shameless, Nameless & Recycled, POP gallery,
　　Los Angeles
Detroit: Breeding Ground, Museum of New Art,
　　Pontiac, MI
Kevin Beasley and Vanessa Merrill, Museum of
　　New Art, Pontiac, MI
:Wellness:, Cave, Detroit
Change: It's all there already, Stamps Gallery,
　　Stamps School of Art & Design, University of
　　Michigan, Detroit

2008

This and There, Somewhere, Forum Gallery,
　　Cranbrook Academy of Art, Bloomfield Hills, MI
Andres Serrano Picks Detroit, Center Galleries,
　　College for Creative Studies, Detroit
Detroit-Toledo Exhibition, Secor Gallery,
　　Toledo, OH
Still Moving, Cave, Detroit
Michigan Fine Arts Competition, Birmingham
　　Bloomfield Art Center, Birmingham, MI
Semester in Detroit Art Show, University of
　　Michigan, Ann Arbor

2007

Stag, Cave, Detroit
Exhibiting Group Show, Detroit Industrial
　　Projects, Detroit
Black and White, Cave, Detroit
Selections IX, Center Galleries, College for
　　Creative Studies, Detroit

2006

*Even Clean Hands Leave Marks and Damage
　　Surfaces*, Detroit Industrial Projects, Detroit
*Selected Works by Deb Garlick and Kevin
　　Beasley*, Neal Davis Gallery, Royal Oak, MI
Black and White, Neal Davis Gallery, Royal Oak, MI

Residencies

Delfina Foundation, London
International Studio & Curatorial Program,
　　Brooklyn, NY
Museum of Contemporary Art Cleveland
Rauschenberg Residency, Captiva Island, FL
The Studio Museum in Harlem, New York

Permanent Collections

Albright-Knox Art Gallery, Buffalo, NY
Art Gallery of Ontario, Toronto
Art Institute of Chicago
Columbus Museum of Art, OH
Dallas Museum of Art
Hammer Museum, Los Angeles
The Institute of Contemporary Art/Boston
Museum of Modern Art, New York
Pérez Art Museum Miami
San Antonio Museum of Art, Texas
San Francisco Museum of Modern Art
Solomon R. Guggenheim Museum, New York
The Studio Museum in Harlem, New York
Tate Modern, London

Exhibition Checklist

Untitled, 2014
Shag rug, polyurethane foam, resin, clothespins, thermal shirts, underwear, and studio debris
80 x 50 x 5 inches (203.2 x 127 x 12.7 cm)
Collection of Lonti Ebers, New York

Untitled (Jumped Man), 2014
Polyurethane foam, resin, soil, coat-sleeve liners, and Nike Air Jordan shoes, size 18
Two parts, each 24 x 16 x 11 inches
(61 x 40.6 x 27.9 cm)
Collection of Miyoung Lee and Neil Simpkins, New York

Strange Fruit (Pair 1), 2015
Nike Air Jordan 1 shoes (white and black), resin, polyurethane foam, tube socks, shoelaces, rope, speakers, hypercardioid and contact microphones, amplifier, patch cables, and effects processors
Dimensions variable
Solomon R. Guggenheim Museum, New York
Commissioned by the Young Collectors Council with additional funds contributed by Josh Elkes, Younghee Kim-Wait, and Julia and Jamal Nusseibeh, 2014. 2014.74

Untitled (. . . just watch), 2015
Nautica rain jacket and resin
37 x 38 x 20 inches (94 x 96.5 x 50.8 cm)
Collection of Brian McMahon, New York

Untitled, 2015
Collared shirts, T-shirts, socks, pants, television mount, and resin
70 x 70 x 16 inches (177.8 x 177.8 x 40.6 cm)
Private collection, New York

Untitled (11), 2015
Altered New Era fitted hats, housedresses, T-shirts, bandanas, studio debris, pillowcases, resin, down feathers, raw cotton, and television mount
94 x 77 x 28 inches (238.8 x 195.6 x 71.1 cm)
Rennie Collection, Vancouver, BC

Untitled, 2016
Resin, canvas, and sweater on canvas
46 x 19 x 4 inches (116.8 x 48.3 x 10.2 cm)
Collection of Claire Oliveira Tavares, New York

Untitled, 2016
Resin and altered sweatpants on canvas
48 x 21 x 5½ inches (121.9 x 53.3 x 14 cm)
Collection of Steve Corkin and Dan Maddalena, Boston

Untitled, 2016
Resin and altered sweatpants on canvas
24¾ x 23¾ x 3½ inches (62.9 x 60.3 x 8.9 cm)
Private collection, Boston

Untitled (Rhythm and Blues), 2016
Resin, housedresses, kaftan, and a
women's wool coat
81 x 23 x 14 inches (205.7 x 58.4 x 35.6 cm)
Collection of the Hudgins Family, New York

Phasing (Ebb), 2017
Resin, housedresses, kaftans,
speakers, and audio equipment
91 x 77 x 33 inches (231.1 x 195.6 x 83.8 cm)
The Institute of Contemporary Art/Boston
Gift of Bridgett and Bruce Evans

Slab (Site/Picked A Constellation), 2017
Housedresses, kaftans, T-shirts, socks, du-rags,
cotton, soil, bandanas, altered garments, altered
fitted caps, and resin
78¾ x 80 x 3 inches (200 x 203.2 x 7.6 cm)
Hill Art Foundation, New York

A view of a reflection, 2017
Housedresses, kaftans, T-shirts, socks,
du-rags, bandanas, altered garments, altered
fitted caps, altered bedsheet, mouthguards,
feathers, and resin
82¼ x 178 x 5¼ inches (208.9 x 452.1 x 13.3 cm)
The Komal Shah and Gaurav Garg Collection,
Atherton, CA

Night of the Avenues (diptych), 2017
Housedresses, kaftans, T-shirts, socks, du-rags,
hair rollers, altered garments, altered fitted caps,
and resin
Two parts, left: 79½ x 80¾ x 4 inches (201.9 x
205.1 x 10.2 cm); right: 79¼ x 80¾ x 4 inches
(201.3 x 205.1 x 10.2 cm)
Courtesy the artist and Casey Kaplan, New York

Push, 2017
Housedresses, kaftans, T-shirts, du-rags,
altered garments, altered fitted caps, pushcart
fragment, and resin
79 x 80 x 3 inches (200.7 x 203.2 x 7.6 cm)
Private collection, Chicago

*If I was standing alone I wouldn't
stand it at all*, 2017
Housedresses, kaftans, T-shirts,
du-rags, and resin
99¾ x 53 x 53 inches (253.4 x 134.6 x 134.6 cm)
San Antonio Museum of Art, purchased with
The Brown Foundation Contemporary Art
Acquisition Fund

Curator's Acknowledgments

I want to express my profound gratitude to Kevin Beasley for his powerful and moving artwork, his commitment to the studio, and his generous and open spirit. Kevin and I met in 2014, when I was coordinating my very first exhibition at the ICA, Thomas Lax's traveling exhibition *When the Stars Begin to Fall: Imagination and the American South*, and it has been a pleasure to bear witness to the development of Kevin's work and career in the intervening years. I am so very pleased to be bringing this book and exhibition to the public.

Kevin Beasley is the culmination of the hard work of many individuals. I extend my heartfelt appreciation to Jill Medvedow, Ellen Matilda Poss Director, for lifting up this project, and to Eva Respini, Barbara Lee Chief Curator, for her steady encouragement throughout its evolution. Jeffrey De Blois, Assistant Curator, provided immeasurable support for this book, exhibition, and related programs over the past year and a half. I would like to thank E. M. Joseph for her careful management of Kevin's studio. Casey Kaplan and his entire gallery staff, especially Veronica Levitt, Jeremy Roby, and Jamie Russell, have been champions of this project and collaborators from the very start. Miko McGinty, Rebecca Sylvers, and the team at Miko McGinty Inc. brought this book together with great sensitivity and design expertise. Donna Wingate supported this book in myriad ways, and I sincerely appreciate her steadfast work and resourcefulness throughout the process. Within the ICA's small and stalwart curatorial department, I would like to thank especially Jack Arbaugh, Associate Registrar; Abigail Newbold, Director of Exhibitions; and Tim Obetz, Chief Preparator, for their patient and able oversight of innumerable details related to this exhibition. The ICA has a dedicated and fearless staff and board of trustees who make our curatorial work much more impactful, and I would also like to thank each of them.

I am honored by the generous exhibition support provided by Fotene Demoulas and Tom Coté, The Coby Foundation, Ltd., and Bernard Lumpkin and Carmine Boccuzzi. I would also like to express my deep appreciation to all who have loaned artworks from their collections, generously sharing them with the ICA and our visitors.

They include Steve Corkin and Dan Maddalena; Lonti Ebers; Solomon R. Guggenheim Museum, New York; Hill Art Foundation, New York; the Hudgins Family; Casey Kaplan, New York; Miyoung Lee and Neil Simpkins; Brian McMahon; Rennie Collection, Vancouver, BC; San Antonio Museum of Art; The Komal Shah and Gaurav Garg Collection; Clarice Oliveira Tavares; and private collections in Boston, Chicago, and New York. I would also like to thank Bridgitt and Bruce Evans, who made it possible for the ICA to acquire Kevin's sculpture *Phasing (Ebb)* for the museum's permanent collection.

During the process of creating this book and exhibition, I was fortunate to meet many amazing individuals close to Kevin who supported our work together. I would like to thank, in particular, Mark Bradford, for his contribution to this book; Loring Randolph, for her insights early in the project's development; Fred Abi-Hassoun, for welcoming us into his store and sharing his family's story; and Kevin's family, especially his parents, Lawrence and Deborah Beasley, and wife, Golnaz Esmaili. A number of friends and colleagues provided advice at key moments: my thanks to John Andress, Dell Hamilton, Africanus Okokon, Alexandria Smith, and Kris Wilton. Finally, I first encountered Kevin's work in an intergenerational exhibition that also included works by artists such as Benny Andrews, Beverly Buchanan, David Hammons, Lonnie Holley, Ralph Lemon, Rodney McMillian, and John Outterbridge, among others. Like Kevin, these artists insightfully repurpose found objects; integrate music, performance, and visual art; and activate collective and personal histories, expanding the boundaries of art and the art world. I am humbled by the perseverance of these and other artists and curators of color, who generate outlets for their creative expression and evolution within a system that is stacked against them, and I am inspired to reform our art world to be more welcoming, sincere, and equitable.

Ruth Erickson
Mannion Family Curator

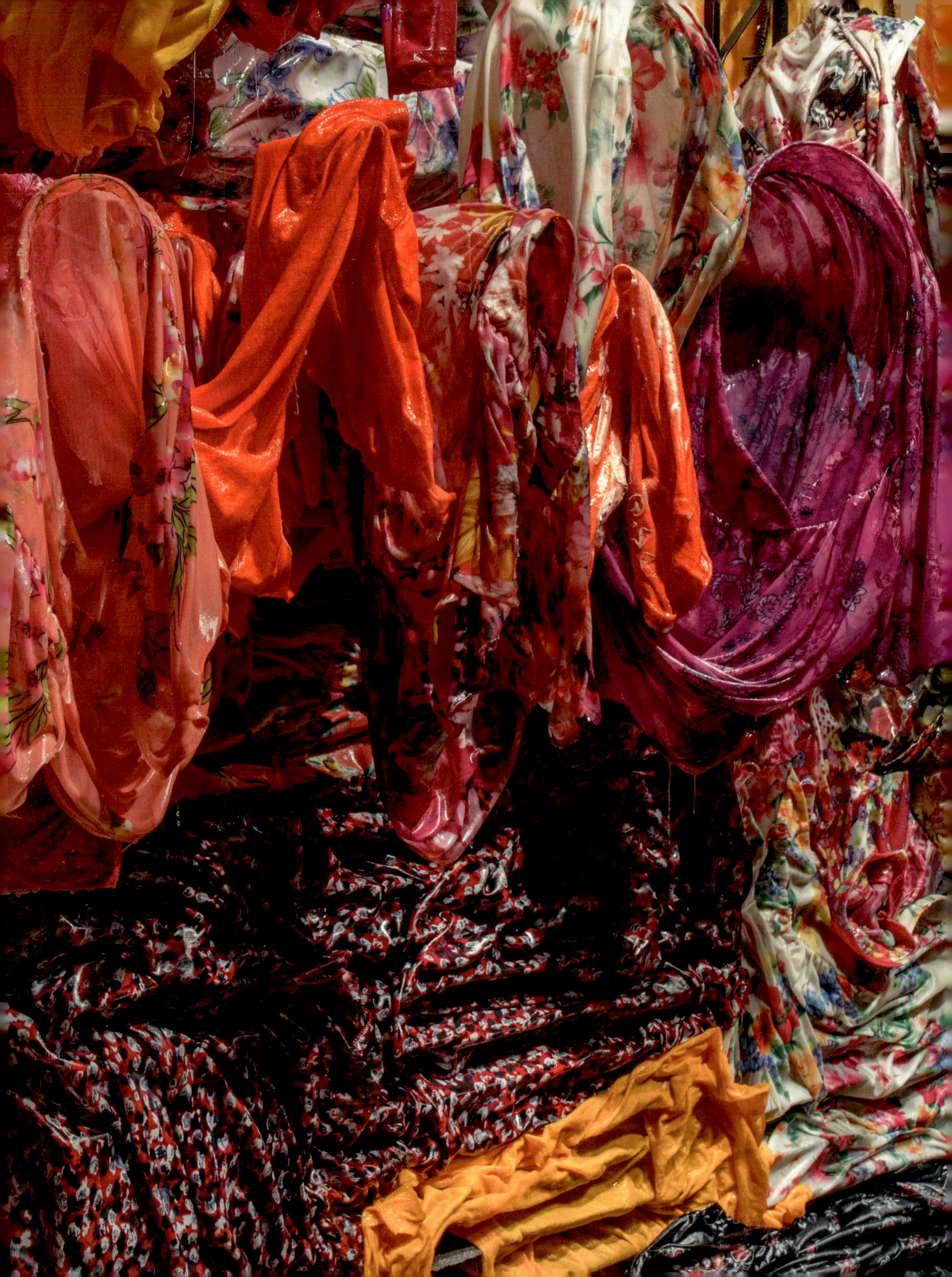

Trustees of the Institute of Contemporary Art/Boston

Chair of the Ministers of Defense (detail), 2016. Installation view, *Hammer Projects: Kevin Beasley*, Hammer Museum, Los Angeles, 2017. Rennie Collection, Vancouver, BC. Photo by Brian Forrest.

This book is published on the occasion of the exhibition
Kevin Beasley.

Organized by Ruth Erickson, Mannion Family Curator,
with Jeffrey De Blois, Assistant Curator.

The Institute of Contemporary Art/Boston
May 9–August 26, 2018

Support for *Kevin Beasley* is generously provided by
Fotene Demoulas and Tom Coté, The Coby Foundation, Ltd.,
and Bernard Lumpkin and Carmine Boccuzzi.

Front cover: *Untitled (11)* (detail), 2015. Altered New Era
fitted hats, housedresses, T-shirts, bandanas, studio debris,
pillowcases, resin, down feathers, raw cotton, and television
mount. 94 x 77 x 28 inches (238.8 x 195.6 x 71.1 cm).
Rennie Collection, Vancouver, BC.

Frontispiece: *Slab (Site/Picked A Constellation)* (detail), 2017.
Housedresses, kaftans, T-shirts, socks, du-rags, cotton, soil,
bandanas, altered garments, altered fitted caps, and resin.
78¾ x 80 x 3 inches (200 x 203.2 x 7.6 cm). Hill Art Foundation,
New York. Photo by Jason Wyche.

Table of Contents: *Untitled* (detail), 2014. Shag rug,
polyurethane foam, resin, clothespins, thermal shirts,
underwear, and studio debris. 80 x 50 x 5 inches (203.2 x
127 x 12.7 cm). Collection of Lonti Ebers, New York.

Back cover: *Untitled (11)*, 2015. Altered New Era fitted hats,
housedresses, T-shirts, bandanas, studio debris, pillowcases,
resin, down feathers, raw cotton, and television mount. 94 x
77 x 28 inches (238.8 x 195.6 x 71.1 cm). Rennie Collection,
Vancouver, BC.

Editorial: Donna Wingate and Marc Joseph Berg/
    Artist and Publisher Services, New York
Publication coordinator: Jeffrey De Blois
Proofreading: Polly Watson
Design and production: Rebecca Sylvers and Miko McGinty
Printed in Belgium by die Keure

A catalog record for this book is on file with the
Library of Congress.

Available through:
ARTBOOK/D.A.P
75 Broad Street, Suite 630
New York, NY 10004
www.artbook.com

ISBN: 978-0-9972538-2-5

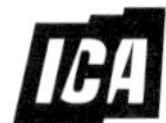

The Institute of Contemporary Art/Boston
25 Harbor Shore Drive
Boston, MA 02210
www.icaboston.org